Volume 1: Getting Started

Decisions Decisions: Getting Answers to Life's Challenges   Large Print

Haneefa Mateen

Copyright © 2023 by Haneefa Mateen

ISBN: 978-1-73772-19-4-9

All rights reserved. No portion of this book may be reproduced in any form without written permission from the publisher or author, except as permitted by U.S. copyright law.

Disclaimer: The author of this book, Decisions, Decisions' stories, experiences and opinions are from author's perspective and are not intended as medical advice or the use of any techniques as a form of treatment for physical, medical, psychiatric, mental health problems either directly or indirectly. The intent of the author is only to share experiences in a general nature in her quest for emotional and spiritual wellbeing. In the event that you use any of the information in this book for yourself, which is your constitutional right, the author and publisher assumes no responsibility or liability whatsoever for readers or purchasers of this book.

Decisions, Decisions is a non-fiction story, however some names, locations, and other identifying information were changed to protect privacy of individuals.

Book Cover art: Haneefa Mateen

Contents

Introduction	1
PART ONE: GETTING STARTED	7
Chapter 1: What are Oracles?	16
Chapter 2: Metu Neter Cards	20
Chapter 3: What's in a Name?	26
Chapter 4: Afrikan Women Warriors	41
Chapter 5: Heru Khuti (Ogun) Clan	49
Chapter 6: Rituals	57
Chapter 7: I Ching	65

Chapter 8: I Ching Destiny Readings	71
Chapter 9: Career Readings	75
Chapter 10: Native American Cards	79
Chapter 11: Medicine Cards	82
Chapter 12: Sacred Path Cards	93
Chapter 13: In Person Spiritual Readings	97
Chapter 14: Cuban Candomble Priestess Consultation	100
PART TWO: GETTING AWAY	110
Chapter 15: School for International Training	111
Chapter 16: The Drop Off	119
Chapter 17: Which Country?	125
Chapter 18: Zimbabwe	129

Chapter 19: Ndebele Language and Culture	134
Chapter 20: Village Life	150
Chapter 21: Purpose for Being in Zimbabwe	160
Chapter 22: Stout?	169
Chapter 23: Moving On	176
Chapter 24: Independent Study: Zimbabwe Healthcare	186
Chapter 25: Traditional Healers	192
Chapter 26: Before Colonization	207
Chapter 27: Personal Reflections and Struggles Living in Zimbabwe	212
Chapter 28: Americans Over Concerned About Cleanliness, Germs and Illness?	222
Chapter 29: Vegetarian Dilemma	230

Chapter 30: Reality of the Situation	245
Books and Articles Mentioned in This Book	251
Author's Bio	258

Introduction

For those who have been frantically worried they are going to make the wrong decision, especially when responsible for other people's lives, this book introduces some solutions. What it is like to have an overall view of what is going on before you make a major decision. If you lose sleep because you're worried that you still don't know your life purpose, natural talents and career yet, there's hope. Hopefully, you are inspired to learn more about your own life purpose, as you follow along my journey with some of the tools and strategies I use to make major decisions, and to learn about myself and my life purpose. Keep in mind, I'd lived half of my life before I was introduced to these indigenous or ancient concepts. In amazement, while learning different cultures' divination and then looked back on my past, what I saw was very accurate. And you will too.

Divination provides roadmaps or a GPS that lets you know where the traffic congestion is and guides you through the detours. Sometimes we get stuck in traffic anyway. GPS gives alerts and warnings ahead of time. Divination also gives you alerts and can help you get back on the main road of your life.

As you start to see less crises in your life, as you understand how the universe functions around you, and make better choices in your thoughts and behaviors, then it is not hard, even for us who are hardheaded, to believe. Especially when your life begins to flow smoothly synchronically, and what you need simply shows up abundantly.

This is not a religious book. It is a cumulation of 30 years of studying and using various different cultures' divination methods. I use some foreign language terms because that is the way I learned them and is my way of continuing to honor these indigenous cultures and beliefs. With deep respect for indigenous cultures and the people who truly have the knowledge, I thank them and yield to them.

Hopefully this book introduces you to different perspectives as my personal stories bring understanding of how ancient and now popularized practices for making decisions — when used properly — brings improved quality of life, inner peace, satisfaction, and sense of purpose on your own life's journey.

My goal with this book, <u>Decisions Decisions</u>, as with my other books in the "Spirituality Made Simple series" is to make spirituality and healing simple. Simple to understand, and simple to apply to daily life. In the first book, <u>Mother's Love from Beyond: A Healing Journey of Grief and Loss</u>, readers learned about my childhood and early adult years, as I was prepared through life experiences to accept that there are many different ways of healing and knowing. Readers gained faith and courage along with me as I learned to trust intuitive higher guidance.

In this book, I offer tools for you gaining access to your own guidance for your own life, while continuing with my stories of how I was introduced to these divination tools and how my life changed along the way. This book is mostly written in the order I learned these techniques however, the stories are updated with my current thoughts, events, and style of writing. Previous readers asked me to go into more details about my middle years, my thirties, forties, and early fifties to explain how I got from, and transformed beyond multiple crises and obstacles from then to now.

I use several approaches to meet different readers' needs, interests, and learning styles. Some people learn best from information and research. Other people enjoy and learn from life stories as examples. Here, both approaches are combined. Take what you need and leave the rest. At different times later in your life you may want to come back to this series for more understanding.

PART ONE: GETTING STARTED

I was first introduced to the concept of oracle cards and divination through an African-centered church, the Ausar Auset Society Church in 1991. They had weekly classes where I learned about ancient African history, philosophy, and cosmology's different ways of viewing the world. They taught us about improving our health because poor health affects our ability to manage our own emotions and behavior. This included spiritual health as we wonder, what's the reason and purpose for living? Why get up in the morning day after day? There's got to be more to life than this? Why does this keep happening to me? Why do I feel so lonely and empty? Why did I keep choosing the same type of relationships, the same dudes?

I had recently married and divorced twice making me feel lost, like a failure, and wondering how not to repeat the same mistakes. I was feeling lost too because since I almost died in 1982, there were several weird experiences that I didn't yet have an explanation for. No one close to me knew of the term "near death experience, and neither had I, until I found the book, <u>Heading Towards Omega</u>. However, although the author's stories told about how people's personal values, relationships, body sensitivities, even personality changes after a near death experience, there wasn't guidance for what to do with these changes. I felt very alone.

In these Ausar Auset Society Church classes, I began to get answers to these life challenges, though I didn't understand much in the beginning, I just followed along. Attendees were instructed to first get a destiny reading also known as an incarnation objective from a priest. A "reading" is a spiritual guidance consultation. The reason for a destiny reading is to learn your purpose for having been born on Earth at this time, and what lessons you are to learn. Later, we learned how to do our own spiritual readings using oracle cards or coins.

These destiny and other spiritual readings are not meant for fortune-telling. Divination is to help you grow emotionally, mentally, heal physically, build a strong spiritual character with responsibility to community, therefore having success with true abundance in all areas of your life. After doing the initial destiny readings, then you can ask about your destiny or life lessons at more frequent intervals such as daily or monthly. Later, you can inquire about specific situations or projects that you are in, or you wish to be involved in. But all readings are to be referred back to your destiny reading. In other words, ask yourself, "How does what I want to do, and the current spiritual reading help me to fulfill my destiny?"

However, over time I did observe some spiritual readings do foretell the future. Initially it was six months, and sometimes ten years later these events would unfold, that helped me understand the meaning of the reading. Being new to doing spiritual readings, I had no idea this would happen. I began to see that spiritual readings predict current and upcoming challenges, and gives advice to assist with navigating personal as well as situations with relationships, family, major purchases, moving, career, employment, and supervisors.

Shekum ur Shekum (Ra Un Nefer Amen), the founder and leader of the Ausar Auset Society Church a Pan-African spirituality church, commented in one of his classes that one day someone should write a book showing how their own spiritual readings and understanding evolved. I was surprised when he mentioned this idea, because he previously taught that what is in each individual's "book of charms" is private. It was emphasized that no one sneak and read anyone else's notebook without permission. However, since I am in my later years of life, and knew several people who came to Ausar Auset Society Church who told me they did not understand and therefore didn't benefit from the teachings or spiritual practices, I've decided to share some of mine. I greatly benefited from Ausar Auset Society Church and it was a springboard for the rest of my life.

You May Be Wondering . . .

Wait a minute! What is it that I believe then? Isn't this against what most major religions teach? Or personal free will and independence? Let me explain. My beliefs changed for me after I had a near death experience back in 1982. Many people are having near death experiences these days, as they are surviving what used to be fatal illnesses such as heart attacks, strokes and cancer, or car and other crashes, drownings, falls, gunshots, fires, floods, tornadoes, and weird accidents. They return to tell stories of meeting with an energy of pure Love, Peace, Acceptance and Infinite Knowledge and Wisdom. They see Angels, their loved ones and others who passed on, that they thought had died. Those who have had near death experiences whether they flatlined, or their car was completely totaled yet they walked away without a scratch, see their whole life flash before their eyes. A life review from birth until now, showed that most of what they thought was wrong, and rules that were broken aren't as important as how they were kind, understanding and compassionate with other people. This helps them see their purpose for living, the need to return to Earthly life to finish what they started, change their thinking and behavior, heal and help others. Then they often choose to come back, or may be pushed back into their bodies to wake up with a commitment to do better. However, they are also told that they will temporarily forget most of the wisdom and personal insight shown to them.

Next time, on my Day of Judgement, during my life review, I want it to show that I learned what love is, how to receive, accept, and share love. That I loved, more than I hurt people, during this lifetime. That I used the talents that I was blessed with. Over my lifetime I've noticed that it really doesn't matter what religion or beliefs that I've tried out, heaven still provides for me with abundance. Perhaps this abundance comes from faith, love, sharing, gratitude and following heaven's guidance.

I've borrowed the good from several religions, beliefs, and theories. Using the example of a puzzle, this is because each culture, society, religion or group has pros and cons with only a few pieces, often missing a lot of the rest of the worldwide puzzle picture. No group sees the whole picture. We need each other. No one has all the answers for the best way to live. Together we can learn, grow and evolve.

Chapter 1: What are Oracles?

The dictionary's definition of oracles is a person who is usually a priestess or priest that is a medium through whom advice or prophecy was sought from God. The word "oracle" is from the Latin verb for "to speak." An oracle can also be a wise person. Sometimes young children bring us important messages.

Closely related to oracles is divination. Divination is the practice of seeking to foresee or foretell future events or hidden knowledge by interpretation of symbolic happenings in nature, or by the aid of people gifted with unusual insight or intuitive perception. Divination is found in all civilizations' histories.

Since most of us are not yet fully open to our own intuition, often too busy or distracted, not having extensive quiet time like our ancestors did to notice the environment around us, therefore using tools such as cards, coins, shells, bones and other assorted items for divination are helpful for getting guidance for life challenges.

What I noticed over the past twenty years is sometimes the oracles will give similar advice no matter what question I ask. This means there is some attitude, thinking, or behavior that I must change within myself before my outer life situation will improve. Changing one's self may take weeks or months, but the rewards with the increased abundance and helpful people in your life is worth the effort.

People often comment that I radiate peace, love, and confidence. The peace comes from doing the inner work of acknowledging all of my feelings including the anger, hurt and sadness because included with these uncomfortable feelings is joy and inner knowing. And from following through on the outer work of taking action based on the guidance received. Knowing that all is in universal order, I am able to let go of worry.

With all the different types of divination systems and oracle cards, what is most important, is whatever you choose is easy to understand and is comforting for you. Having good books for interpretation is essential. So I have about four I Ching books, and a few oracle card books. There is a list of some of the ones I use at the end of this book.

Chapter 2: Metu Neter Cards

The first oracle cards I learned were the Metu Neter cards that were designed by Ra Un Nefer Amen. These are seventy beautiful cards with colorful pictures representing the ten Kamitic African deities on the Tree of Life plus four other energies that influence our personalities and life events. What I liked about Ausar Auset Society Church teachings is that "deities or gods" are not up in the sky somewhere, they are qualities, talents, and abilities we each have inside us, in varying amounts. We can make the decision, conscious and unconscious through meditation and actions to improve our thinking and behavior to meet whatever challenges we have in life. Instead of, "this is the way I am, or "I've always been like this," or "this is the way I've always done it," or "how my grandpa did it."

It was freeing to learn there are infinite possibilities. Otherwise, I grew up like most people, feeling inadequate and stuck.

When using the Metu Neter cards, besides asking "Please give higher spiritual guidance, insight into understanding this situation and what I need to do, I also add "what energies are needed for this situation? Then based on the specific card, I listened and meditated to the mantra on the 30-minute cassette or CD. I would sing the mantra aloud or in my head during the day, and especially in the situation I inquired about. I wore the special colors, ate the foods with the energy of the deity, and did my best to emulate the positive attributes of the deity pictured on the one or two cards I selected.

For detailed explanation and instructions refer to the book, <u>Metu Neter Metu Neter Vol. 1: The Great Oracle of Tehuti and the Egyptian System of Spiritual Cultivation</u>.

After saying a prayer asking for guidance, the first question I asked was about my destiny. I pulled the Het-Heru Hetep card. From the book and classes, I learned that with a Het-Heru destiny throughout my life I should strive to be joyful, to experience pleasure in healthy balanced ways, be sociable, harmonious with others and nature, and appreciate the beauty in all. Further, I'm to be aware of how I use my imagination in my thoughts and daydreaming fantasies as these could come true in life.

Strong inner joy and pleasure raises the life-force which will inspire and motivate me towards passionately fulfilling my goals. Best to decrease tendencies to be timid, seeking too much pleasure, wanting to feel good all the time by daydreaming or using intoxicating drugs, alcohol, sex and other addictions to avoid unpleasant tasks and responsibilities. Careers to consider are all kinds of artists: dancers, musicians, singers, writers, entertainers, make-up artists, fashion designers, interior decorators, drawers, painters, graphic designers, and animators. Het Heru is also known as Osun in the Yoruba traditions.

Some of these Het Heru traits I already naturally had. My mother was an artist and introduced me to drawing and painting at a very young age. As she read us storybooks, I was inspired to dream of becoming a children's book illustrator. Family said my mother was famous for her singing. An elementary school teacher told me I had a wonderful singing voice, but I was too shy to get up in front of a classroom, so certainly not for an audience. During my teen years, I designed and sewed clothes and dolls, and drew pictures in solitude. As an adult, I love to dance, occasionally until 4 o'clock in the morning at non-alcoholic parties. People who observe me move, tell me I am a natural dancer.

Het Heru's day is Friday. So on Fridays I do creative art activities, put on music and dance, get out in nature, call and do fun activities with friends. My money donations are usually multiples of $5. I also do Het Heru meditations and purposely eat sweets on Friday's.

Chapter 3: What's in a Name?

Next we were instructed to select an African Kamitic name that expressed the values of our individual Metu Neter destiny card. I initially choose Hetep Ab Meri-t which means having a peaceful, joyful, balanced heart. I selected other names, but this is the name that received a positive Metu Neter card verification to help me live out my Het Heru Hetep destiny whenever anyone says my name. Then in 1993, the <u>African Names,</u> book came out, and in a naming ceremony the author and priest Hehi Metu Ra Enkamit gave me a different name AkhiaNeter-t. Akhia means joy and Neter means

God. The "t" added at the end makes it feminine. All together AkhiaNeter-t means "God is my joy." The priest told me, "This name will remind you to raise your inner joy to match your smile."

In my first book, <u>Mother's Love from Beyond</u>, I wrote about the many meanings I learned about my legal name, Haneefa. My mother told me Haneefa means "inclined to righteousness." Name books and the Internet say it means "true believer."

A taxi driver gave me a different interpretation than I had heard before.

He said, "It is faith so big, huge, like the faith of Abraham"

This is true. Over the years, my faith increased as I've delighted in miracles happening alongside challenges, usually after I've bravely persevered. His interpretations of my name Haneefa matches my African Khametic name AkhiaNeter-t meaning of God is my joy.

Saturday Born

So how did I start out with a name that depicts such responsibilities of devotion and sacrifice? Perhaps because of the day I was born. The day on which you were born describes more of your personality than your astrological sun sign. It is how people actually see you and how you operate in the world. You can go on the Internet to find what day of the week you were born on. Simply type in your full birthdate then "day of the week." There are sometimes printed perpetual calendar charts available to do hand calculations to determine what day.

Born on a Saturday, and during a Saturn Period meant most of my middle to later childhood was turbulent, with constant relocations and separations from my family. These challenges made me quiet, observant, a loner, with a patient determined focus on meeting future goals. I learned to patiently sacrifice and do without, because my family was poor. I like to spend time with older people listening to their stories, and I have had more maturity than my chronological age.

Naturally organized, I return whatever I use to its assigned drawer, shelf, or same spot on a table so I can find it later. The clothes in my closet are arranged by color on colored hangers, which allows me to easily wear the appropriate color for each day of the week. Turquoise blue on

Mondays, reds on Sunday and Tuesdays, golden yellow Wednesdays, light blues on Thursdays, bright green and yellow on Fridays, and black on Saturdays. Similarly, as much as possible I also eat the foods of the day based on energetically hot and cold foods. My panties are still folded six inches the size of a dollar bill, and my bed sheets have mitered hospital corners from what I learned in Air Force basic training forty years ago. I make "to do" lists and use alarm clocks and timers. Calendars, I write on them but afterwards rarely look at calendars, perhaps because I've had a good memory and internal sense of time. Doing all this doesn't bother me, as it simplifies and makes life easier and convenient. Someone else would be frustrated. Not me.

Het-Heru's personality traits are the opposite of Saturday born. Het-Heru is outgoing, friendly, social, freely sexual, having to be around people, partying, spending money on beautiful clothing, makeup, hair, home, car and fun. On the contrary, I save my money and pay bills to keep a roof over my head. People I've observed with predominant Het-Heru traits, tend to put pleasure first before responsibilities. Although, I do like nice things, I'm more practical.

I learn from mine and other's mistakes, therefore I may be more cautious than other people. And my ability to change, adapt to situations and do things differently than other people who find it easier to just follow the crowd, doesn't make for me keeping many friends or having fun.

What I buy usually have to be practical and have a functional purpose too. You won't see me in miniskirts with my boobs out because I don't like being cold, or my thighs sticking to burning hot wet sweaty chairs, or my back hurting from trying to keep my legs closed. Nor will you see me in high heels hurting my toes, back, making me afraid I might fall on the ice, or couldn't get away if chased! Makeup, whenever I could find shades that matched my brown skin tones made pimples with painful white pus filled boils on my face, and lipsticks gave me an itchy blistery puffy lips. Lipstick for African Americans never made sense to me anyway because our lips are already full and beautiful. Our legs are naturally tanned, so why wear odd-colored hot, itchy stockings? Contrary to television commercials' guarantee that fingernail polish would make our fingernails stronger, my fingernails split and break each time I use fingernail polish. When I was a teenager, I begged my parents to get my ears pierced but no one told me I could be allergic to cheap metals until my earlobes immediately swelled. Luckily I was able to keep the holes in my ears. Occasionally, my ears still protest with hypoallergenic earrings. If men only knew the pain we women go through to look "pretty." Burning scalps with hot combs or perms, early balding from hair dyes that never matches the God given color and texture we were born with. Sitting for hours getting extensions of someone else's or fake hair weaved in.

Like excuse me, is the only way I'm beautiful is to look like the actresses and other female entertainers on TV and other media? With straight hair and red lips from the 1930's and 1970's?' Betty Boop?

The way most women wear makeup doesn't make sense to me, except of course to cover scars from pimples, blotches and discoloration. Eventually, I did find hyperallergenic makeup, and with the help of a young friend, we bought some from Macy's department store. Sometimes I used a pink lipstick and fingernail polish that's closer to my natural skin color. To me, makeup should enhance each individual's natural features of own shape of face, skin tones, and hair. "Extreme makeovers" on television? How is that a makeover, if everyone comes off of the stage looking the same? The same haircut, same streaked hair color, and same make up as the stylist gave the woman before her?

The only reason I might consider makeup is due to my age, my hair everywhere is thinning. You would have to look hard to see my eyelashes. Penciled in eyebrows and eyelashes frequently turn out cartoonish. Or like I had a good cry. Why do boys and men have the long eyelashes without even trying! Surely they must know girl's eyelashes don't grow like that. But maybe salesmen do know. And that's why they persuade women that something else is wrong with them. Here's another product to buy that keeps businesses' bank accounts looking pretty. Me? I'm done with making everyone else rich but me! Besides, if men are not naked or hurting themselves to look pretty why should I?

This is my practical Saturday born energy thinking. Perhaps I'm too practical and frugal for my own good. But my destiny reading is to be more like Het-Heru, how do I do this?

What did I know about romance? When I was married, my husband took me out to dinner. He ordered the lobster, salad, baked potato entrée for the both of us. Sitting in a dimly lit corner at a table just for the two of us. From the window we could see the calm water and boats docked on the river. Quietly enjoying talking and laughing.

That is until when the waiter brought the check and I saw the bill – $32 — and as my husband pulled out a big wad of dollar bills, I yelled at him.

"Do you know how many groceries we could have bought for that much money?

And after you take the shell off, for a little bit of fish and only one baked potato! And don't carry around all that money in your back pocket!"

I embarrassed him (and myself) as I continued to fuss at him on the way out the door.

Well, I never had lobster before. Nor had I been to an expensive restaurant before. I didn't know that's what couples do as a treat on special occasions, when he takes her out and pays for the meal. Not grateful he would spend that much money and time on me. (Back in the 1980's that was a lot of money).

Honestly, I do try. Just prior to the COVID-19, pandemic crisis, I was doing more socializing. I bought pretty clothes, was giving more attention to my hair, and discovered one day that I needed to clip the long gray hairs on my chinny chin, chin, that probably everybody else noticed but me. Now I clip these little hairs twice a week on Monday's and Thursday so I remember.

Socializing? It seems there are always situations that are perfect excuses for not fulfilling our destinies. Throw in using a wheelchair so can't get in most people's homes to visit. Apartment buildings usually have walk-ups with several flights of stairs, as do party venues.

For Het Heru, true beauty comes from within. Joy and peace glows outward. I've actually experienced joy after doing Het Heru meditations, rituals, or more often after simply experiencing fun or witnessing amazing beauty, and especially after healing past traumas therefore freeing me of worries.

Apparently I glow. Unconsciously aware of this wonderful energy men flirted with me, sometimes using vulgar language, ask to marry me but just met me, told me how beautiful I was, even complemented my fingernails. Actually this joyful, loving energy is what everyone wants to have. But this has to come from inside yourself and lasts longer when it is real. Can't charm or steal joy from others, expecting to keep it for yourself. As usual, I wasn't wearing makeup nor fingernail polish on my short length, clipper trimmed fingernails. So other than my gorgeous smile that people tell me I have, what was the sexual physical attraction?

Another example of the how the day of the week you were born on might be influencing your life or people you know I will explain using the popular movie Black Panther.

Chapter 4: Afrikan Women Warriors

There are some people who expressed disagreement with the portrayal of strong women warriors using martial arts and weapons in the movie, <u>Black Panther</u>. This discontent was stated by men and women. However, if we understood indigenous cultures before colonialism, we would not be surprised, or be caught up the current controversy over the demand for non-binary and transgender identities to be recognized. Let me explain this further from my understanding of indigenous African perspective that I learned in 1991 from the Ausar-Auset Society.

West Africa has the tradition of naming children by the day of the week they are born on. These natural personality traits occur regardless of gender. In addition, everyone has all of the abilities of all of the seven days of the week within us, just on varying amounts with some traits more natural than others. So, we really should not be surprised when a mother sees her child in danger then suddenly has the incredible strength to leap across the street in a microsecond or lift a two-ton heavy car off of her child! Or to fight off an attacker! Or a father to tenderly understand and nurture a sensitive child! Over time we have gotten away from being fully present in our bodies, aware of our environment, and connection to self, community and the universe for guidance. Guidance that would intuitively give us the ability to do whatever needs to be done in the moment.

The day of the week you were born is also the clan that you would be assigned to in the village. This way everyone is valued and needed. No clan or personality traits are any better or worse than another clan. Not like European or capitalistic societies who promote everyone has to be a doctor, lawyer, or computer geek to be successful and accepted! The example I like to give to describe how everyone is necessary is when the village decides to have a party or celebration. The clan that would head up the committee would be those born on a Friday, who are the natural partiers with the natural ability to have fun, bring people together in harmony, are the artists, musicians, entertainers, and decorators, with beautiful clothes, makeup, sexy and sensual, to make sure there is dancing, wonderful food, and soothing beverages. However, Friday born people like having fun, but are not into doing hard work. They would need Wednesday and Saturday born people to help with logistics, financial planning, and audio-visual technology. Thursday born people who have the faith and optimism and ability to bring wealth and make sure the event is spiritually correct. Sunday born people to take the lead in delegating responsibilities. Monday born people for cooking, nurturing, dedication, and dreaming the party into being. Tuesday born people for security, the bouncers for when people have had a bit too much partying.

So yes, Tuesday born people no matter whether they are male or female would be the warriors and protectors of the village! They would be trained from childhood to be warriors and protectors. They have the natural ability to see the overall situation, analyze and strategize what needs to be done. The warrior personality is not necessarily aggressive. However, if fighting is required, so be it. Most of the time though, the warrior clan is tasked with upholding the laws of Maat. This requires being honest, speaking the truth no matter what -- hurt feelings or not. They are fearless, adventurous risk takers. They do not tolerate injustices. Tuesday born people's job is to help the village let go of what is obsolete and move on to what is required in the new current situation. They are pioneering and innovative. Most other people are reluctant to change, even if it is for the better, so there can be a lot of arguments. This is a "masculine" or yang energy" that allows us to follow through on our goals. The warrior women in the movie, "Black Panther" fearlessly stood up for their community, and with the laws of Maat announced the community came first, and then those that were physically able, yes, with martial arts and weapons fought. The Maat principle inherited in Killmonger and the other African tribal leader guided them to eventually put the future of the African nation first, although by Western standards this would be considered "weak," "soft" and "feminine." We know it as balance. The balance of masculine and feminine energies within all of us and for our communities' wholeness.

Another of the African-centered contradictions with Black Panther being one of the Avengers, is the use of brute force and fighting as a way to settle disagreements and to establish dominance. Even who was to become the king of Wakanda was decided by which brother killed the other brother. This is not the traditional African way. Kingships and other disputes were settled by consulting with the elders, the ancestors, and God through the use of trance and divination wisdom systems using cowrie shells, bones, and other sacred items. Personal opinions, emotions, and consensus were not essential for decision making. A better perspective would be gained through divination consultation to know who was most suited for a position, what was needed for the current situation, what may happen in the future, and the consequences of wrong behavior. Therefore, higher guidance was sought for impartial decision-making for the higher good of the entire community. Much could have been learned by all from both Killmonger's and T'Challa's initial return. In addition through consistent spiritual practices, the priests and priestesses would have already known ahead of time the father would be murdered, that T'Challa and later Killmonger would be coming home to Wakanda and would have prepared for these situations.

Chapter 5: Heru Khuti (Ogun) Clan

The other influence on my personality, that is the opposite of Het Heru's sweetness and dislike of any argumentative confrontations, is my moon sign. The planet that the moon was in at the time of your birth, also describes more of your personality than your astrological sun sign. My sidereal moon sign was in Scorpio which is a Mars energy. Although some computerized charts indicate a Sagittarius moon, I was born in the wee hours of the morning in the darkness of the night, while the moon was still in Scorpio. Mars is a warrior energy. West Africans would say, Ogun. Ancient Northern Khametic Africans would say, Heru Khuti warrior energy.

"You don't look like you are in the Heru Khuti clan."

I smile. Quiet, with a charming smile instead of a menacing frown, I understand why people would ask, "You? In the Heru Khuti clan?" and laugh. They didn't see or hear of me loudly arguing, starting fights, or going around making trouble. Always slender, I didn't appear to be able to beat people up.

It was from classes taught by Ur Aua-t Sha-t Shemsut, the Queen Mother of the Chicago Ausar Auset Society Church community, I learned the more subtler characteristics of Heru Khuti as a fearless, risk taker. The fact I was there in the class, having rode a Greyhound bus or Amtrak train, got on subway trains and buses to travel to the Southside of Chicago was a hint. I'd been on New York City subway trains too. Never even occurred to me to be afraid until my brother said, "You were on the subway in New York? Don't do that again!"

A brief fear came over me, as I briefly remembered the movies and news reports of people being robbed or stabbed in the subway. But wait a minute! I hadn't seen any violence on the buses and trains in Chicago nor New York. Yet, in my brother's and my hometown, I saw a man grab a purse from a young woman sitting in the front of the bus behind the driver, then run out the door. She began sobbing and wailing, "He took my insulin. He has my insulin. What am I going to do?"

Occasionally, there were fights on the buses, but I'd seen none of this violence in the big cities. For years, I worked night shift, occasionally second shift, and even on dayshift having to be at work by 7 AM, it was dark going to and from work. I simply said a prayer and kept going. What's there to be afraid of?

Self-disciplined and focused, it is easier for me to immediately stop a behavior or habit cold turkey whenever I learned that it is wrong. Or I would steadily work hard to change over a few months or year. This takes courage and perseverance. You will certainly risk losing relationships, because close family and friends are used to you being the same. I'm always learning, growing, changing, and on the move. No one knows what I will do next, including myself!

Only another Heru Khuti person can be with a Heru Khuti person! That's what Ur Aua-t Sha-t Shemsut taught us. Their blunt, at times brutal honesty keeps away those who don't want their feelings hurt. Listening, I hadn't thought of myself that way. I do believe it's fairer to gently tell people privately to help them rather than joining others in talking behind their back. I don't tolerate injustice especially when watching others being mistreated. Therefore, people are shocked when I do speak up. Did I say "gently?" The wrongdoer(s) often wished I had argued, yelled and cussed at them. Instead, I simply tell the truth of the situation of what I observed.

They become hurt and angry, frequently avoiding me afterwards.

In the past, I gave people three strikes of disrespecting me and then I left. Took my few belongings and left. Not caring about what I left behind because my freedom and dignity was more important than the stuff or invested time I accumulated. And sometimes I've also left people behind, like I did two husbands.

Herukhuti's role is to point out what is obsolete, no longer useful, even old traditions and to pioneer new better ways of doing. However, many people are reluctant and afraid to change. This is where I've gotten in trouble with leaders in communities and organizations. "We've done this for years. Why can't we just keep doing it this way?"

Over the years, I've toned this tendency to criticize down a lot by telling myself it is their organization, they have the right to do what they want with it. Except when it comes to injustices, then I speak up. This is also why I rather not belong to any one organization or religious group. Now that I'm older, I have stayed longer. Can you imagine? Some places I've stayed 10 years or more. Hard for me to believe this myself. Sometimes you have to be a part of the change you want to see in the world.

Heru Khuti children often get a lot of beatings and punishments. Not so much because of their impulsive, exploring and experimenting but because they know when their parents are lying, are unfair or being hypocritical by telling the child not to do something but the parents are doing it. They will fearlessly argue with their parents and teachers. My stepsister told me that when I was little, I had a reputation for not being disciplined and was like a wild child, according to my stepfather. Maybe, maybe not. Most of the beatings I remember receiving from him was because his rules didn't make sense. He would accuse me of lying when I told him, I honestly didn't do what he wanted to punish me for. Previously, my mother bragged that I was not a good liar so I'd already given up trying to lie. My defense was to not cry. Just stand there and look at him. It didn't make sense to me, to mentally accept punishment for what I did not do.

Chapter 6: Rituals

All African descent churches, yes even CHURCHES use music, the rhythm of the preacher's voice, tambourine, drum going faster and faster until lured into a peaceful trance until you feel like getting up dancing. Filled with the "Holy Ghost" from Gospel praise songs extended longer and longer and longer. In Africa, and elsewhere, African spiritual religious rituals it is the same, except everyone is up dancing and singing.

Each month, Ausar Auset Society Church's classes taught us about a different deity from the nine Paut Neteru deities on the Tree of Life. Auset, Sebek, Het Heru, Heru, Heru Khuti, Maat, Tehuti, Sekert, and Ausar. Each deity symbolizes beliefs, personality traits and behaviors that everyone has within self. The goal is to have the ability to change and do what is required for whatever the specific situation and challenges life presents us with. During the specified month we did our best to personify the deity's good qualities, wore their colors, ate their foods. In addition, we each did our own individual oracle readings on what to personally focus on throughout the month.

On the full moon we came together in an African style ritual, singing the deity's mantra and dancing to their specific drum rhythm. This was similar to the music on the meditation cassettes and CDs but was much more powerful live. The combined group energy and music took me easily into trance. Initially, the priest and priestesses were astonished at my ability to dance and easily go into trance, since I had not been exposed to African traditions before.

Ausar Auset Society Church doesn't do animal sacrifices for rituals. Instead, each individual is encouraged to sacrifice problem thinking and behaviors and replace it with better understanding and appropriate behavior for a better self, family and community. The following example is what I gained from a Sebek ritual.

***

Sebek (Elegba) Ritual

Sebek is described as a dog, a clever fox or coyote. The priest instructed us to see ourselves as having the head of a dog as we danced to the sound of the drums and Sebek mantra being sung. Many indigenous traditions have a trickster or joker to get us to laugh at our own foolishness. Sebek had me laughing as I saw myself as a dog digging and digging long tunnels outside at night, looking for my bones. An image of my checkbooks came to my mind. At home I couldn't find my checkbook for weeks. I intended to tuck it away safely but somehow hid my checks from myself. Usually I know where everything I own is, because I have a designated place for each item where I consistently return it. I couldn't even hide money from myself. Other people are happily surprised when they find five dollars or $20 in their pockets. Not me.

At the time, I was a roommate with someone whose son often had parties with his friends in our absence. I'd return to see people had been in my room and slept in my bed without even the courtesy to make it up before they left. On the other hand, at least then I knew someone had been in my bed. But this wasn't the first time, that I had misplaced checks. Hid them from myself, thinking I was putting them in a safe place. It happened twice, years before when I tucked my income tax checks away, even forgot about them until I found them a year later. I had to call the IRS and ask if I could still cash it! They luckily said, "Yes." Sebek's number is three. This was the third time this happened to me, so obviously I still hadn't learned my lesson yet. I was going overboard with trying to feel safe, but was it true? Perhaps I was only tricking myself. Realizing this while in trance, I laughed and laughed vowing to let go of worries. Later that week, I found my checkbook.

The unseen healing energies from the Ausar Auset Society Church group meditations and rituals gave me some of the incredible inner love and peace, I had longed for since during my near death experience in 1982, when I experienced Oneness with total love, peace, acceptance and understanding. I repeatedly prayed asking, how can I have this inner peace in Earth life? I felt driven to heal emotionally from past traumas and grief, after trying to push away the grief feelings by working hard in college and on the job didn't help. So I tried different types of alternative psychotherapy modalities. Then in 1991, I discovered the Ausar Auset Society Church meditations, yoga, healthy Ayurvedic diet, homeopathy and rituals healed my emotional distress, toned down my psychic empathic sensitivity, so much so, I no longer needed traditional talk psychotherapy.

A note on animal sacrifices: killing animals have a different meaning and reverence for cultures who herd animals for food and wealth, than for U.S. Americans who think their food comes from the local grocery store, and children believe money is free from ATM machines. My mother used to ask me when I was a child and begged her for money or items,

"What do you think? Money grows on trees?"

What may be a sacrifice, emotional, or financial hardship for one person may not feel like a sacrifice for someone else.

Disclaimer: What I write here in this book about Ausar Auset Society Church's teachings is from my own understanding and perspective. Much has probably changed in the 20 years I've been away from Ausar Auset Society Church.

Chapter 7: I Ching

The second divination method I learned was the I Ching. My first I Ching reading was, of course, for getting more understanding of my destiny life lessons. Initially, a teacher showed me the book, <u>The Illustrated I Ching Workbook</u>, which uses a simple method using three cleaned regular pennies method for determining the six lines of an I Ching reading. Other books' methods require mathematical calculations. You throw the pennies or I Ching coins gently onto a tabletop, then write down either a straight line or a broken line to indicate yang or yin lines. You do this three times, pause, leave a space, and then throw the I Ching coins another three times to get the upper second trigram. You use the chart in the back of the books to determine the numbers of the combined six lines, that make up the hexagrams.

In a short time, I began to love the I Ching as a way to receive guidance from God. This is because the I Ching explains the overall situation. Perhaps it is problems with the supervisor, or a business's finances, or business practices or national or global economic or political influences. Sometimes it is not the right time to do what you are inquiring about. For me, knowing this was a great relief. Through religions and schooling, we are so used to thinking that each of us personally is to blame, when what we trying to do encounters obstacles. Instead, the I Ching helps us remember there is a larger world around us. Many happenings in the environment influences our lives, which we are unaware of, and couldn't have control over. This allows me to let go of worries and be peaceful knowing that there is truly a divine plan, and all will be well.

From I Ching classes, the book, <u>The Harlem River Arrangement: The I Ching Transcripts</u>, by Ra Un Nefer Amen, and personal experiences I learned there are up cycles and down cycles in life. This means there are months or years when we have more energy to do activities than at other times. For example, similar to the seasons of the year, we are less likely to feel like doing a lot of work in the winter when it is very cold or in the summer when it is very hot. On long summer days we would harm our health working from sun up, to sun down especially in the heat. Additionally, we extend the day even longer with artificial lights, air conditioning, and heating in the winter. Our businesses, schools, and extracurricular recreation activity schedules demand continuous productivity year-round, without regard to the changing seasons or individual needs. Pushing and pushing our bodies, yet somehow, not expecting our bodies to break down and demand a rest from all the overthinking and exhaustion. An I Ching message will warn us when we need to rest.

The other observation is the I Ching would sometimes give me the same hexagram or another hexagram with similar interpretations no matter what question that I asked. After a while I understood it meant the message was about me. Therefore, I needed to change my behavior or my thinking. Soon, there would be situations to test and challenge me. For example, the instructions may be to be quiet and patient, but I felt frustrated, righteous, and wanted to advocate. The I Ching may indicate it is a situation where those in charge aren't able to change yet, won't listen, nor understand. Therefore, I would be wasting my time or even making the situation worse. Then there are times when the message is, I do need to speak up but I am afraid or tired, or I don't know how. The I Ching gives me the encouragement to learn how.

The book Ra Un Nefer Amen published in 2014, <u>I Ching Praxis: Forty Years of Practical Insights into the I Ching</u>, in my opinion doesn't have the spiritual depth of his class lectures. Well okay, the title does say "practical." This opinion of course is based on my comparison to his previous book, <u>The Harlem River Arrangement: The I Ching Transcripts</u>, which is all I knew when I started.

Chapter 8: I Ching Destiny Readings

My I Ching Destiny Reading

Hexagram 34 (lines 3 and 6) into Hexagram 38

Hexagram 34 Power of the Great. Has a potential for great strength and power. However, I'm being warned there is danger of me relying on my own willpower and forgetting to ask what is right and fair before proceeding. May tend to push forward without waiting for the right time, and to see the overall perspective of the situation. Need to persevere with patience and calmness.

Line 3: gives the image of a goat butting its head against a hedge, and getting its horns tangled and stuck in the branches. Well, my mother did say I was stubborn and hardheaded when I was a young child. And that I did actually used to bang my head!

Warns against pushing ahead anyway thinking and boasting you can do it.

Line 6: The goat is stuck and can't go backwards or forward. So eventually relaxes, considers its mistakes and yields. Therefore, good fortune as now are able to go forward.

Hopefully, will evolve to being able to let go of feeling the need to always defend yourself and be so stubborn because of fears and being insecure.

Hexagram 38 Opposition can lead to misunderstandings and disagreements. But opposites are natural dualities that often causes us to reach out to others to seek union.

Later, after the class was introduced to the book, <u>The Astrology of the I Ching</u>, I learned there are more ways to obtain an accurate I Ching destiny reading than just throwing the coins. Here instead your destiny is based on your birthdate, location and time of birth. The book has complicated math and charts for determining your birth hexagrams as well as degrees of auspiciousness or good fortune. Again, each hexagram describes the best personality qualities to aspire to as well as possible weaknesses and troubles in your life. Decades later with the invention of the Internet and ability to google anything, there are I Ching websites that will do the math calculations for you. Gratefully, I discovered my math was all wrong! And stunned with mixed feelings in 2021 when I read the correct destiny hexagram, that I will discuss later on in Volume 4, Chapter 16. For now, learn along with me.

Chapter 9: Career Readings

The next important spiritual reading you will want to know, is what your career path should be. This is what I got for mine in January 1993.

Geb tem tchaas/ Amen hetep. Hexagram 40 Deliverance (lines 2, 3, 5, and 6) into hexagram 33 Retreat. Geb means physical health or the health of the situation you inquired about. It also represents the physical world and material needs. At the time I did this reading I was having problems with asthma.

Hexagram 40 Deliverance as obstacles, difficulties and tensions are beginning to be resolved. Return to normal life as soon as possible but don't overdo. Correct and forgive mistakes.

Line 2: By developing one's own inner strength and correctness this helps overcome obstacles in public life caused by those persons wrongly placed in official positions.

Line 3: When going from poverty to experiencing comforts, have to be careful not to go beyond one's means or usual personality and position.

Line 5: Have to leave behind people that are doing wrong. This means mentally letting go too.

Line 6: There is a person in a high social position who is wicked and preventing progress. He should be forcefully removed.

Hexagram 33 Retreat. It is best to retreat from the situation temporarily. Meanwhile prepare to return later.

October 1994. What energies are governing my career this incarnation? I forgot I already did this reading the previous year. At that time, it was my understanding it was only to be done once in a lifetime. Breathed a sigh of relief later when learned you can do career readings as needed. Nonetheless, this is the answer I received:

Metu Neter cards: Tehuti tu tchaas /Tehuti tem maat.

Hexagram 58 The Joyous represents true inner joy. Joy along with gentleness and friendliness influences other people.

However you shouldn't get caught up in excessive amusement, charisma and social pleasures.

Since I was just beginning to learn about the I Ching, I didn't know yet what these hexagrams meant.

Please Note: The I Ching interpretations and insights came from reading several I Ching books, listed in the back of this book, which I used to summarize the main points here and in later chapters.

Chapter 10: Native American Cards

Medicine Woman Cards

A friend, Anna asked me if I wanted her to do a reading for me. At that time, I didn't know of any cards except the Metu Neter cards. I accepted my friend's offer of advice because of curiosity and I didn't know what I was going to do with my life. Having withdrawn from art school because it was too expensive and was about to resign from a minimum wage job working in the deli kitchen of a natural foods store, I didn't know what to do next.

The seventy-eight cards set Anna used was the Medicine Woman Tarot Deck. It came with a small paperback, <u>The Medicine Woman Inner Guidebook: A Woman's Guide to Her Unique Powers Using the Medicine Woman Tarot Deck</u>. Ann pulled the usual three cards for past, present and future, the Pierced Shield, Eight of Arrows, and the High Priestess Seeker: Inner Reflection/Wisdom cards. I made brief notes from what she read to me, however after all these years, I only remembered the turning point guidance and that I needed some R&R (rest and relaxation/ recreation). Both the past and future cards Ann pulled for me mentioned "turning points" especially my future card the Seeker: Inner Reflection and Wisdom card.

I went home and followed the instructions to make a list of what major events happened every seventh year of my life from when I was seven, fourteen, twenty-one, twenty-eight, and thirty-five years old. The major events could occur a year before or after.

7 years old: My mother married my stepfather and we moved to a city in another state.

14 years old: Sent to foster home at age 13.

21 years old: Air Force. Married.

28 years old: Near-death experience at age 26. Graduated nursing school at 28. Divorced at 30.

35 years old: Joined a new religion. Moved to Chicago to go to art school.

Chapter 11: Medicine Cards

Another friend, Paula, and I went looking for the Medicine Woman Tarot Deck at the Healing Earth Resources bookstore. The store didn't have it. So instead, when we found among many other cards, <u>The Medicine Cards: The Discovery of Power Through the Ways of Animals</u> book, we each bought a set. The original card deck had forty-four cards and was later expanded to fifty-two cards.

***

Another Destiny Reading: My Nine Totem Animals

The behaviors and attitudes of these nine power or totem animals represent abilities, talents, and challenges you have had throughout your life since birth. Some abilities still need awakening and developing, yet the potential is here. Connecting to these nine power totem animals in each of the seven directions East, South, West, North, Above, Below, and Within will help with understanding the lessons of each direction. To learn about yourself and for a detailed explanation and instructions refer to the book, <u>The Medicine Cards</u>.

East: Butterfly/Transformation. The East direction represents accepting guidance for our greatest spiritual challenges and illumination. I gasped and briefly sobbed as I read the interpretations for both the Butterfly and the Snake Cards because these accurately described the past 40 years of my life. It seemed I was continuously in the process of some type of transformation. The butterfly metaphor was my inspiration to not go backwards when life got tough, because it's not possible anyway for a butterfly in the chrysalis stage to go back to be a caterpillar. Plus I've loved butterflies, embroidering, painting, and drawing butterflies to me.

South: Snake/Transmutation. The South direction is our childhood trust and innocence that needs to be protected. People with true snake energy medicine are considered rare because they are able to symbolically go through multiple snakebites, being poisoned, shedding one's skin and still survive and thrive. Healing on all levels physical, mental, emotional and spiritual. Although you can fear changing one's being and life situation yet again because change can be uncomfortable, you know this won't last long. Ongoing life-death-rebirth cycles. These transmutations bring about the ability to create through enhanced psychic, sexual, and spiritual energies. Having survived childhood abuse, domestic violence and ongoing racism it felt like I was getting bitten again and again. Therefore, it's been hard for me to trust other people and my talented abilities.

West: Grouse: Sacred Spiral. The West is our ability to be introspective going within to know own personal truths, answers and goals. Grouse symbol of a spiral brings awareness of personal power. In meditation, visualize yourself spinning in a spiral pattern towards the center. This reminds me of how children love to spin yet don't seem to get dizzy. In high school modern dance class, I learned to spin without getting dizzy by looking at a specific chosen spot on the wall with each turn. Nowadays I can spin with my eyes closed, and when opening them occasionally but not fall down. The Sufi whirling dervishes spin in a spiral circle that brings on a state of ecstasy when they connect to the oneness of the universe. Dancing is another way to ground myself because I can be too much in my head daydreaming, mostly problem-solving and analyzing. Grouse also symbolizes death and rebirth! (groan). Sekert too.

North: Turkey: Giveaway. The North is wisdom gained. Turkey is an acknowledgment you have transcended the self. To now be able to be of service to others. Turkey energy medicine is similar to the principles of Maat that I learned from Ausar Auset Society Church: sharing, helping others knowing we are all one, that what you do for others you are also doing for yourself. But not to give to receive. Knowing heaven always provides for all — gives inner peace, faith and optimism. No need to want and hold onto stuff or talents you aren't using that someone could make use of. Willingly give away what you are not using.

Above: Hummingbird: Joy. Above us is the Great Star Nation from where we

came and will return. The attributes are very similar to those of Het Heru/Osun. Pure inner joy and love, spreading joy with your presence, along with harmony, and an appreciation for outer beauty. Hence, I was given a Khamitic name meaning Heaven is my joy.

Below: Antelope: Action. Below is the Earth, the Inner Earth. The importance of being connected and staying grounded with the Earth. Antelope energy medicine gives mental clarity and physical strength with the ability to make quick decisions and take action to get tasks done. Antelope provides guidance and solutions when we listen and act. Have the courage to trust and speak truth, being willing to go a new different way instead of automatically following others. I did mostly listen and follow my intuition. What I needed in order to follow through, synchronistically showed up: the money, time, the information, and people to help. But I was timid in groups and institutions about doing things differently. I would speak up but if leadership kept doing routines as usual, I followed too. Most initiatives I did in the privacy of my own home.

Within: Swan/Grace. The Within direction symbolizes your own heart's joy and your own personal space within and around you. You have a choice of what and with whom to share your personal thoughts, energy and space. Be faithful to your own personal truths. Swan energy is being able to accept a greater divine plan and going with the flow. It is the ability to go into the dream time, with different levels of consciousness to know the future. Again more transformation and healing as a result. For me, that means when I feel sleepy, to stop doing whatever I'm doing, take some deep breaths, perhaps a little nap, and also reminds me to meditate regularly. Accordingly, when I need to be fully present and accounted for, Swan energy reminds me I need to do regular grounding exercises to connect with the Earth. And to know the difference between what it feels like to be grounded versus daydreamy.

Right Side: Elk: Stamina. The right side direction protects our masculine side similar to how a good father would. It gives us our courage and warrior energy. Elk represents stamina which is increased by pacing yourself, although this may take longer to accomplish your goals, you will be less likely to become burnt out. Elk is also having companionship with those of your own gender. In my case sisterhood. On the other hand, Elk is doing activities with the opposite gender because it is important to have a healthy exchange of masculine and feminine energies.

Left Side: Coyote. The left side direction protects your feminine side. The feminine qualities of receiving abundance and nurturing and connection in relationships for yourself and others. An appreciation of mothers.

Coyote is the infamous trickster. But most of the time we trick ourselves. When we don't learn from our mistakes, or self-sabotage and fool ourselves by not facing the truth of how we really feel with the present situation. Coyote gets us to laugh at ourselves. It can also warn us somebody else is trying to deceive us. However, I wondered how coyote traits would protect my feminine side? So I pulled another card asking for clarification. Dog: Loyalty. Dog medicine energy is loyalty. Being able to serve others and humanity and explore deeper ways to serve. Being loyal to friends. Yet maintain allegiance to your own personal truth. Thank you Sebek!

Chapter 12: Sacred Path Cards

Later we discovered there were spreads in the Medicine Card book that used both the Sacred Path Cards and the Medicine Cards. We decided to buy the Sacred Path Cards too. The Sacred Path Cards became my favorite cards. I prefer the <u>Sacred Path Cards: The Discovery of Self Through Native Teachings book to the Medicine Cards</u> book because the accompanying Sacred Path stories explain the Native American spiritual teachings in an easy to understand way. Therefore, easier to apply to my everyday life.

One of the first Sacred Path cards I pulled was the 1 Pipe: Prayer/Inner Peace Card. It reminds us of personal responsibility for creating one's own inner peace or discord that flows out into the world. We radiate the feelings and thoughts we hold inside whether we say or act on them or not. We can make the choice to aid world peace by healing our own inner conflict, hatred, doubt or anger. At that time, I had a lot of sadness and loneliness.

In 2009, I found the Sacred Path Cards Workbook. It has questions to ask yourself. Now, I use it more often than the initial hardcover book that came with the forty-four Sacred Path cards. The workbook has additional card spreads for specific questions. However, I rarely do card spreads. One card is challenging enough to understand and live out in everyday life!

Combination Readings

I began adding both the Medicine Cards and Sacred Path Cards to using the I Ching, when I did my every six months' solstice readings on June 20 and December 21 each year. Sometimes the I Ching only has one hexagram with no specific line stressed to help me know what information applies to me. Similarly, if I pulled only Uatchet or Nekebet cards from the Metu Neter cards deck. With time I saw that the Sacred Path cards with additional other oracle cards helped me understand both the I Ching and the Metu Neter readings much better.

After a while I stopped using the Medicine Cards because I was rarely out in nature to connect with animals to follow through with the recommended exercises. It was even difficult to visualize my totem animals. This made me feel I wasn't honoring the Native American culture. Whenever I do encounter a bird or animal, then I pull out the Medicine Card book to read the interpretation.

Usually I only pull one card from a deck instead of doing the additional card spreads of laying out three, five, ten cards, or more. For me, it is much easier to understand and follow through on lifestyle changes with just one card. Otherwise it is not possible to remember all that information anyway. Plus, I'm not purposely using the cards to predict my future. I prefer to help influence my future by taking it one day at a time, in the present.

Chapter 13: In Person Spiritual Readings

It was 1991. I was riding home in a car with an elderly couple when I felt such an intense sense of panic and fear I could barely breathe. Soon after I arrived home and got into bed, the phone rang. It was my grandmother Mother Dear, "Your father passed away. His heart gave out."

He died at 11:00 PM, the exact time when I was feeling panicked.

A few days later, feeling lost and confused as I sat across a small table in front of a man dressed in a white robe, and white trousers with a white cloth hat on his dark-skinned head. Nervously I looked around, waiting, in a large room with white walls, I've never been in before. I didn't know what he was doing as he silently tossed some small white seashells on the table. When he spoke, he advised me what to do for my father.

"Hang three bananas at the top of a doorway in your home. Leave it there until the bananas fall off by themselves. Wear bright blue clothes."

I didn't understand most of what he said or why he wanted to me to do such strange things.

Yet, he told me after he tossed and moved around the cowrie shells again, "I can't advise you about your life. You already know what I know."

Huh? What did I know that he knows? From the little he told me, I assumed this meant the wisdom he had. I was only 35 years old at the time. What did I know? Later I learned he was a Yoruba Babalawo priest. He used the cowrie shells or coconut shells to do Ifa divination readings.

Chapter 14: Cuban Candomble Priestess Consultation

On a fall day in 1995. I waited in the living room, with comfortable couches and chairs surrounded by full bookshelves. I kept myself occupied with the book, <u>Light Emerging</u> while subtly listening and observing comings and goings of people in and out of the other room. My friend who invited me, sat next to me. We chatted occasionally but I was nervous not knowing what to expect. I'd paid my fifty dollars ahead of time. After, approximately an hour my name was called, and I was led into a small room where sat a young man and an older woman. He was her interpreter. She introduced herself as Valdeci, then asked my birthdate, wrote notes then proceeded to throw an assortment of small items, shells, and rocks inside a box lined with a red cloth. She gave me a piece of paper with the following:

1st Orisha: Osoosi

2nd Orisha: Osala

3rd Orisha: Oya

The only Orisha that I was familiar with is Oya. Oya is a Yoruba name with attributes similar to Sekert.

The priestess explained to me, " Oguna rules your head. Ogun is the Yoruba name for warriors who in Africa carries a machete or sword. However, after coming to the United States, living among the Native Americans, then Ogun began using a bow and arrow instead. And his name became Osoosi. You are very spiritual. Osoosi's job is make sure your spiritual path stays clear and straight. But this is a double-edge sword. Anything or anyone that gets in the way must go. Therefore you have suffered many losses. From here forward you will have minor difficulties. Your finances will clear shortly. You will find the right job. But you must first lay the foundation, to plan spiritually and materially. Stick to your goals. You must find and follow your own path. Put spiritual first. Health will improve as your spiritual is healed. She gave me cleansing herbs with instructions to mix them with water, and then pour them over my head while I'm standing in the bathtub. Based on the reading from her throwing the items in the box, she said, "I will pray for you but I can't tell you what to do. You already know."

She then asked me if I had any questions. I asked about my mother, where she might be. The interpreter hesitated for a long time and only gave me a few words compared to all the the priestess was telling me. They argued a little between them. Basically he told me, "Your mother is still alive but it will be very difficult to find her. You may not be able to accept the conditions she is in. Some people may not want to be found."

Similar to the previous Ifa reading by the Yoruba Babalawo priest in 1991, again I was told that she couldn't tell me what to do, because I already know what these priest(ess) knew. But how can this be? I still felt as lost as I did four years prior! I'd dropped out of art school and was working at a health food store as a cook in the deli section for minimum wage. A far cry from my training as a nurse. Depressed with severe chest pains with exertion, as well as while sitting, I don't know how I had the strength and the will to continue to be on my feet all day lifting heavy pots, cooking and serving customers, putting away supplies, washing dishes and mopping floors. Plus walk for one hour home and walk another hour back to work Monday through Saturday because initially I didn't have money for bus fare. Perhaps my smile got me through. But is that all I got for my fifty dollars? I needed answers and guidance for what to do next with my life.

Well, on the positive side, at least I didn't have to do similar to some of my friends who went to the same Candomble priestess and had to pay hundreds of dollars to buy an animal to sacrifice along with continued consultations with a priest. A true precious blessing, and thinking about it now, as I write this, still brings me to tears because what the priestess explained to me immediately brought comfort, calmness and healing to my heart. I cried when she told me about Osoosi, because this helped me understand why I had so many losses in my life. Over time I had become hurt and bitter. It was a big relief to have this explanation and meaning. I could stop blaming myself and others, and instead open to forgiveness.

After my consultation with the priestess, I of course went searching for information about who are the other two Orisha, that she told me ruled my head were. Osala is a Spanish language variation of the Yoruba name for Obatala. It is somewhat similar to the Khamitic description of Ausar. That's why the Babalawo priest who did my Ifa reading told me, I should wear white, and whenever he saw me afterwards, he would actually prostrate himself prone on the floor straight out in front of me. Since this was my first reading and introduction to African spirituality, before I went to Ausar Auset Society Church, I didn't understand.

At a local African American bookstore, I found a small book, <u>Ochosi, Ifa and the Spirit of the Tracker,</u> about the story of Osoosi. Spelled and pronounced "Ochosi." It seems when you have strong Osoosi energy ruling your life you will frequently get hurt by and suffer the most losses from the people closest to you. His own grandmother killed his pet bird because she was hungry, after a month with very little food. This parrot was his companion helping him hunt for food in the forest. His grandmother wasn't thinking of the consequences, nor of the special close relationship Ochosi had with his parrot. She only thought of her own needs. There's more to the story.

Ochosi had other skills and talents besides hunting, I witnessed and understand as similar talents unfolded in my own life. In later chapters, you'll learn more of what I learned.

Ochosi energy may have had influence over the Muslim name my mother gave me. Later, I learned that my name Haneefa means more than "inclined to righteousness" as my mother told me or "true believer" found in name books and on the Internet. A university student from Saudi Arabia told me in 2010, that the word "hanif" means "straight, to straighten what is crooked, and to divert something back to being straight or to correct it."

My mouth dropped open, but I didn't know if I could tell a Muslim what I'd been told by a pagan priestess, so I didn't. Osoosi's job is make sure my spiritual path stays clear and straight. How is it I would be told similar meanings by different approaches, languages, countries, religions and cultures? My mother requested my name from a Muslim leader in Pakistan. Perhaps he used astrology to determine which name to give me. Aries is ruled by Mars the warrior. But where did the predicted spiritual abilities come from?

PART TWO: GETTING AWAY

Chapter 15: School for International Training

By 1996, I could no longer tolerate the concrete jungle of being surrounded by tall apartment buildings in Chicago. Initially, I thought this need to be out in nature was because when I was a young child my mother frequently took us to the large city parks. As an adult, I too spent time in parks. However, although Chicago has large parks, it also has a larger population hanging out in the parks, making having privacy rare.

In my meditations and whenever I closed my eyes, even momentarily or before sleep, I would see the beautiful bright vivid fields of red flowers I'd seen when I was on the Other Side during my near death experience. Seeing the red flowers immediately filled me with love and calmness. After a while, I began to want to go, to wherever in the world those flowers may be. In addition, I saw myself in a valley between steep tall mountains with occasional waterfalls. It was peaceful there too, so I began to desperately pray to go to both places.

During the School of the Art Institute's orientation in 1994, I learned about their student study abroad programs. Previously, traveling did not seem like an option because I thought only rich people traveled to other countries. A year later, before almost dropping out of the school because it was way too expensive,

I inquired about the study abroad program when the spiritual group that I belonged to was going to go to Ghana in Africa. Couldn't I finish my bachelor's degree abroad? The Ghana study abroad program focused specifically on Ghana's art history, seemed ideal. Disappointedly, she explained that it wasn't an option because it was an exchange student program, meaning students from Ghana would have to come in my place and that was not likely to happen, unless they were rich and could support themselves without working in the United States.

She showed me the School for International Training's had study abroad programs in over forty countries to choose from, including Ghana. Tanzania had the tallest mountain in Africa, Mount Kilimanjaro. Kenya was nearby. The tuition with scholarships and loans would pay for my year on campus with room and board, and include the flights to and from a country, during my senior year.

As I usually do oracle readings for major decisions, especially considering moving to another state or country even if temporary. I used both Metu Neter cards and the I Ching coins for guidance and insights into the situation:

What energies are needed to be successful at the School for International Training (SIT)? Metu Neter card: Herukhuti hetep. Being courageous, hardworking and fair to others will help remove obstacles.

And then later, "What is my purpose or goal for being here? Metu Neter card: Maat tu tchaas/ Amen tem maat. To have an optimistic sharing attitude, and to learn to let go of old conditioned behavior patterns.

I Ching: hexagram 13 (line 3) into hexagram 25.

Hexagram 13 Fellowship with Men. Focus is on maintaining relationships and friendships with the need to continuously cultivate one's own emotional and spiritual growth to have patience and understanding with others. To be able to transcend one's own fears, selfishness and unreasonable expectations. Most of all, we must strive for higher spiritual clarity, a unified universe as guided by oracles, being open and honest, towards what it means for everyone to be treated equally.

Line 3: May have mistrust and difficult getting along with others, especially when there are differences in perspectives. Being defensive brings humiliation.

Hexagram 25 Innocence. Our true nature is inherently good, especially when we are connected with our divinely guided intuition, inner peace and joy. Success, if don't try to be other than authentic self.

I decided to enroll in the World Issues Program at the School for International Training. It had a bachelor completion program with the junior year on campus, then the senior year away, usually in another country, or in the United States for international students to do independent study. All of the classes offered were so interesting it was difficult to choose only three classes for the first semester from either Population Studies; Peace and Conflict; Community Society and Development; Human Ecology; or

Economics concentration courses. I did I Ching readings on each class to decide but I won't be detailing them here now. The classes I chose were Population Studies; Human Ecology; and Peace and Conflict. All students were required to take the Intercultural Communication class along with some brief introductory economic, grant writing, and teaching English as a second language workshops. The next semester I took the second part of each course: Women, Health and Development; Mediation Skills; and Human Ecology.

As I looked at the teacher at the chalkboard and then around the room at my new classmates, I realize I've seen all of them before – including the teachers. But how could that be? Half the class was from other countries, and the other half of the twenty-six students were from other states. The international students were two from Cambodia, two from Zimbabwe, one from Kenya, one from Eritrea, one from Germany, one from Ecuador, three from Japan, and one from Taiwan.

Chapter 16: The Drop Off

We were only on campus for three days when our teachers explained to us that we would be going to visit nearby Vermont towns. A van would come at 9:00 in the morning. I thought we were going together as a class. However, they informed us that students would be dropped off in pairs or trios in separate towns. We were each given a roll of Lifesaver candy and a five-dollar bill. The van will return at 9:00 the next morning. As the van drove off, Sara, Chifen, and I stood on the corner looking around us at the very quiet town with only a few people walking on the streets. Who could we even ask for help? It's good we already had breakfast, but five dollars wouldn't buy lunch let alone dinner! We walked a little way but then decided to sit in a small park in order to not draw unnecessary attention to ourselves. A Chinese, African American, and white young women in a state whose population was ninety-nine percent white. We nervously joked about it.

As the sun began to set, we started to worry. Where would we spend the night? We still hadn't eaten, and it was dinner time. Across the street from the park was a small church. Together we decided to go knock on the door. The pastor invited us in. His family lived in an attached house. We sat at the table with them as his wife served us a casserole for dinner. Then off to church we went! Not quite what we bargained for. The pastor had already preached to us during dinner, and he continued preaching to us after church while we were preparing for bed, then during breakfast the next day. He yelled at me for doing my usual daily morning Tai Chi. He didn't want to expose his children to anything else but fundamental Christianity, and that's why they home schooled them. He was preaching nonstop to an atheist, a Muslim and a Buddhist! We ran out the door after breakfast. Our ears full, we were glad to get away. Relieved to see the SIT van on the corner.

The School for International Training Campus is located approximately 5 miles away from downtown Brattleboro, Vermont. Our classes were in large houses, as were our dorms, therefore giving us a family style community feel. Even the newest building with the cafeteria looked like a large house. Alongside the paths and roads were bubbling streams, waterfalls, and wooded areas. Surrounded by rolling hills, the hills looked like mountains to me. I loved hiking through the woods and up the hills. In the fall, the bright spectacular colors of the autumn foliage was breathtaking. We often had classes outside while moose looked on.

"Mud season? What's a mud season?" I asked.

I guess I should've known the answer, because the pretty white boots that a friend gave to me, became brownish as my feet got sucked in with each step in several inches of snow. Hey, who could complain? I'd truly gotten away from the tall concrete apartment buildings and skyscrapers of large cities.

A Different Perspective. While I was at a bookstore in downtown Brattleboro, I found another I Ching book, <u>I Ching: a New Interpretation for Modern Times</u>. Reading this new version of Hexagram 34 Great Strength made me feel much better about my incarnation destiny reading. I learned I have lot more influence on other people than I ever thought. Having grown up with a lot of criticism by my fathers and from negative racial stereotypes by others, I was a quiet introvert. Protected from the streets, I always felt I had to catch up with everyone else. I wondered why anyone would pay attention to me. Still hexagram 34 warns me to not to take advantage of people using my influence.

Nor ignore I do have influential power. My lacking self-confidence, awareness and social skills would have people confused and bring them down. Being more outgoing than usual would actually give other people strength. This was a surprise to me. Line 3: cautioned me to not become overconfidence from past successes, and to not try to force situations.

Chapter 17: Which Country?

During the School for International Training's application process, potential students were asked to list three countries they wanted to go to and with short essays explain why. Of course, I couldn't say it was because I saw visions of fields of flowers, mountains and waterfalls. I had to learn more about each country.

To decide, I inquired of the oracles about Jamaica, Australia's aboriginal culture, Kenya and Zimbabwe. Zimbabwe was the best reading. I actually cried because I hadn't heard of Zimbabwe, didn't know anything about it. Later when I went to the library to do research, I calmed down when I saw Zimbabwe actually did have fields of flowers because the Dutch grew and exported tulips from Zimbabwe. It also has the enormous, famous Victoria Falls. In addition, I was interested in indigenous medicine and Zimbabweans often go to traditional healers. Since I was a registered nurse, I wanted to study healthcare systems.

Deciding whether to go to The School for International Training's College Semester Abroad Program:

Metu Neter cards: Sebek tu Maat/Het Heru hetep. Some of Sebek's attributes are travel and education.

I Ching hexagram 37 (line 4) into Hexagram 13. Line 4: Great good fortune and well-being when expenditures and income are balanced. In public life, this is the person whose sharing benefits the general welfare of all. Again hexagram 13 counsel on how do I make and maintain friendships with people whose culture is different from mine?

Zimbabwe Organization Rural Association Progress (ORAP) SIT Study Abroad Program?

I Ching: Hexagram 21 Biting Through (lines 5 and 6) into hexagram 17 Following. Hexagram 21 is about removing obstacles to unity in the community because of someone's misbehavior. They will need correcting or punishing. Each line of the hexagram helps determine whether the penalty should be mild, harsh or severe.
Line 5 is more about the judge

being too lenient with punishment. Line 6 is a person who's behavior is incorrigible and they need to be removed from the community and denied privileges. Hexagram 17 Following: is when someone more experienced helps someone less experienced. Usually this is an elder helping. Learning to share and serve others. It also means following the natural cycles and laws of the universe.

I decided to go to Zimbabwe anyway, although I didn't understand who's behavior needed to be corrected, but I was encouraged by the I Ching changing into a positive situation if there are elders there to assist.

Chapter 18: Zimbabwe

After a sixteen-hour flight from New York, we stayed the night at a hotel in Johannesburg, South Africa before flying to Bulawayo in the morning. Resting in bed, whenever I closed my eyes, I saw red flowers with green leaves. I thought, as I looked at the bright vivid colors behind my eyelids that I must be getting close to where there will be endless fields of flowers like I seen for years in meditations and dreams.

Upon arrival in the city of Bulawayo, I observed the scenery from the van's windows. The land seemed semi-desert with green cactus plants that resembled aloe vera. It was the end of winter in the Southern Hemisphere, so there were miles and miles of bare short trees with crooked limbs. The houses had stucco on the outside in various colors of white, tan, blue, green pastel colors. Most of the houses had small gardens surrounded by red dirt. In spite of the bare trees, there were large bushes with beautiful bright red, light or hot pink flowers. Perhaps in the spring after the rains, I will see the endless fields or bushes of real red and other color flowers.

Synchronistically I was led to choose Zimbabwe. Soon after coming onto the ORAP Zenzele College campus, I suddenly felt like I've been in this area before. The way the air felt, the furnishings even in the bathroom and kitchen. Very peaceful, safe feeling atmosphere. Perhaps from memories of my great aunt Lil's farm, when I was a little girl, where my family stayed for a few weeks each summer. Maybe my history goes back much further. It was an overwhelming peaceful, yet confusing feeling because somehow, I could just be with these intense feelings, while in a group of mostly young white women who were in the habit of talking and moving constantly. I could not explain my awe, as I looked at the shrines in each corner of the large room, and one in the middle of the room divider composed of small pebbles on the bottom, then somewhat larger stones on top of that, and large red stones topping the whole pile. At the base of each of the corner's shrine were also gray pebbles, an old wooden stool, a wood shelf covered by a long-draped cloth hanging from the ceiling. On the shelves were intricately woven baskets that appeared empty, and other assorted unfamiliar items with a different colored cloth made each shrine unique. One shrine was draped with a long string of leather medicine bags strung close together.

I looked at the ground outside, saw the red soil and burst into tears. I felt like I had come home. This was confusing to me because my family did not come from down south in the United States, and I don't remember seeing red soil before. I had only heard about it. In addition, slaves weren't known to come from southern Africa. Whatever the reason, I had an overwhelming feeling of being home.

The Second Drop Off

Ten days after arriving on the ORAP campus, the van dropped us students off in a rural village for our first homestay. Being on campus, in a small city neighborhood, despite being in a foreign country was familiar to us. Our dorm building had twin bedrooms, washing machines, dryers, and hot showers. The rural villages did not. No paved roads, no electricity, no indoor plumbing with running water to sinks nor toilets. Houses were round, colorful, but small. Very few people spoke a even a little English. Scared, in shock we were immediately immersed for three days in different languages and customs.

Chapter 19: Ndebele Language and Culture

While I was waiting to go to SIT, I went to the downtown Chicago public library language department and asked for audio cassette tapes and manuals for learning Shona. Later, in Vermont on the SIT campus, there was no one who spoke Zimbabwean languages so I chose to continue learning and improving my Spanish from classes that I had many years ago in high school, because every student at SIT had to pass a foreign language fluency qualifying test in order to graduate. In the ORAP semester abroad program I was surprised I had to learn another new language. I did not know there were two major languages in Zimbabwe. Shona is spoken predominantly in the north and Sindebele in the southern region of the country. Ndebele peoples originated in South Africa when it was Zululand. The invading colonizing British unfortunately privileged the Shona peoples over the Ndebele people. Therefore, books and newspapers were written in Shona or British English.

We learned more about Zimbabwean culture and customs in the Ndebele class on campus than the language. Each student had an interpreter in the villages who tutored us. There were times when we were out in the villages for weeks more than we were on the ORAP campus in the city of Bulawayo. For class events, there were a few different interpreters, besides the one that I was personally assigned while I was in the village. Some words didn't translate directly to English. People seemed to talk for 30 minutes, yet the interpreter would only give me two sentences. Is it because Ndebele is more of a story language, that I seem to hear the same words being repeated by the person who was speaking? Maybe the interpreter wanted to spare me the repetition. The reverse happened in the first village I went to, where I would say several sentences and interpreter will go on and on and on in.

It is true there was a lot of repetition in their explanations and storytelling resulting in long conversations. It took a lot of patience to faithfully listen, and when I happened to drift off, I noticed it was possible to return to listening in at a later time, and understand the main point. They would question me to hear if I understood. If I missed just one word, I had to be prepared to hear the whole explanation all over again! This happened whether they were speaking Ndebele or English. Later interpreters explained that indeed the thirty-minute conversations they translated into English in ten minutes, was because they did reduce the repetition.

The problem, I learned later was also because of differences in cultures, beliefs and points of reference for the topic that was being discussed. Especially when the topic was about health or more abstract spirituality. It was hard work to ask questions for interviews, be understood or to understand answers. When I asked the seeming simple questions, the elders would give me the entire history of the situation surrounding the inquiry from its inception to hopefully the present. I then had to pick out the answers I needed for my independent studies report, from within their story. I learned a lot of interesting information from stories that would last a day or two. However, only a few sentences pertained directly to my initial question. The elders had incredible memories for specific details and were impressive oral historians. I wrote abundant notes. And I decided then, that in the future, I would love to help people write their oral histories.

Ndebele is an expressive language, with the whole body used to tell a story or to express strong emotions. Hands, arms and facial gestures move constantly while speaking. In addition, Ndebele has clicks where you have to use different parts of your mouth and nose to make sounds similar to the Zulu language of South Africa. The villages I stayed in are located close to the South African border. There is also a form of sign language used at a distance for signaling a commuter omnibus minivan, which resembles a taxi and to find out what direction a vehicle is going for example. Whistling is used to call people from a distance. Names are sung within the whistle sound. It is also used to give commands to children and domestic animals.

The other language I hadn't expected to learn is British English. Words spelled or pronounced the same in British English, but have a different meaning than in the United States. Some examples: napkins or nappies are cloth diapers for babies, pigeon-holes are individual mailbox slots, and surgeries are doctors' outpatient clinics. Knocked off is when you leave work at the end of the day, retrenchment is when you are laid off or fired from a job. Somewhat similar to American English words are: a sugar basin is a sugar bowl, a lay-by is layaway credit at store, a jersey is a sweater, Scotch is plaid fabric. Humorously, an eraser is a rubber, the hood of a car is the bonnet, and the trunk is the boot of a car. Chronometer is a clock or watch. Men will be offended if you said they were wearing the pants, because pants are thought of as the little panties for women. Even more confusing is the word trousers isn't even in the British English dictionary.

Zimbabweans commented that I looked like an African (after acquiring a very dark tan from walking in the bright sun), until I opened my mouth and talked, then they realized that I was an American.

Men and women shake hands when initiating greetings. The handshake has three parts: first the fingers, then the thumb, and palm as an American handshake, and then the fingers again. Depending on how familiar the person is with you or when meeting for the first time, the length of the handshake can vary from a brief touch of the fingertips to wondering when the other person it's going to stop the sequence. With friends, the handshake can begin with a near-miss handslap.

Compared to the American way of maintaining eye contact, the

Zimbabwean eye contact varied from none at all, where the only way I would know that two or more people were talking to each other was from observing the sound of their voices. Or very intense staring, making me uncomfortable as they questioned me about my appearance.

All the while I was in Zimbabwe, I felt whole for the first time in my life, because I could be myself. It was wonderful to be surrounded by people of my own skin color. The Zimbabweans were open, honest, and still had their innocence. By innocence, I mean since most people in the villages did not go to school, the natural affection, honesty and intuition that children have was not taught out of them. Boys more than the girls go to school because parents cannot afford education for all of their children. Yet everyone there has a Ph.D in comparison to what we actually learn in United States' schools. Starting with the babies who crawl outside, exploring, intimately getting to know the rocks, soil, and the plants, instead of only reading about rocks. Zimbabwean know the weather and have incredible hearing and eyesight. With no street signs to guide them they can see many miles away. Zimbabweans use whistling with different codes to communicate to people and animals at a very far distance. They rely on each other with farming, harvesting, and building homes collectively as a community.

Students returned to ORAP Zenzele College campus for two months of classroom instruction, reading and writing assignments. Then in October

1997, students in groups of two or three were sent to separate rural areas for our village field studies. They sent me alone as the only African American. We toured nongovernmental organizations and observed grassroot development projects.

Women in the Nkanyiso sewing project group explained to me how they begin to work together collectively:

"Before independence we had some problems concerning life. There was severe drought and famine. In the past days, they were not so smart and had no money to buy clothes. Children were sometimes naked. We didn't know how to make our homes beautiful or even clean. Because of poverty we could not send our children to schools. We had no money for school fees.

So unlike now, back then we were not loyal to each other. We were not working hand-in-hand with each other. So people would just suffer in their homes without going for assistance from neighbors. As a result of children not going to school we are still suffering. If children were educated, they would support the elders. Usually a child is depended on us until 15 years old. Later the elders also depend on adult members of the village. But now adults are unemployed.

Before independence we lacked knowledge of collective working, but after independence we came together to discuss our matters and concerns of poverty and wealth at home. In this case, a woman could share ideas with her neighbors. They found they could start by planting tomatoes and sell them to generate income to support their families. After selling tomatoes we look at each other's families to see which family suffered the most, and then use the money to assist that family to buy food. From the success of this collective approach, we continued to use this method and to improve on it. We also discussed how to build our homes, so they look beautiful, how to keep our homes clean, and each woman then did similar to their own homes. We worked as a group to build each home. Also at this time, we discovered we could use clay to build our homes. These beautiful houses made of polished clay appears to be built of cement, but it shines. Then looking at their beautiful kitchens, we realize we were lacking plates. So we came together and put our money together to buy say for Mrs. K ten plates, then the next time Mrs. S ten plates, etc. until all of us had enough plates. The whites saw us working together and were attracted to learn how we worked too, and they even helped. With working collectively together, everyone realized that everyone is equal. No one is better. No looking down on anyone."

ORAP teaches and promotes the revival of the concept of amalima, which means people meeting together and working collectively, loving each other, with unity of purpose to pull together not only their labor and resources but also their thinking to solve daily problems. Traditionally they used to work collectively with plowing, planting, harvesting and were encouraged by ORAP to extend this cooperation to work together to solve all problems in the community.

From my observations and experiences in the rural villages, collectivism was still very much deeply rooted in the culture. So much so as an American, I felt very overwhelmed and culture shocked over the loss of my individualism that at times I felt I had to defend, yet felt left out of family and community activities, because I naturally was not a part of the group thought processes. So ingrained was my colonized, privileged conditioning of selfishness, entitlement, and narcissism I wasn't really aware of my dumb individualistic thinking and behavior back then.

Their young African men were more mature than American males because everyone in the family has responsibilities from a young age. Gratefully, missing was the competition, low self-esteem, edginess, and the palpable constant anxious tension of sizing each other up behaviors of men in the United States, although Zimbabweans also went through colonialism, apartheid and a recent Civil War. They had only had their independence for fifteen years, when I was there in 1997.

Chapter 20: Village Life

The people of Gwanda came out to greet me upon my arrival, welcoming me saying, "We are glad our daughter has come home."

Women took terms being interpreters. They served me plenty of food and very tasty greens. There was open expression of unconditional love and nurturing with both men and women, even with strangers. Where, as you're talking to someone walking down the road or the street, they will hold your hand whether you are male or female. With the same innocence when a child holds your hand. Nothing sexual. Just that you care and like that person in that moment. They frequently held hands as they talked and walked together. Without the fear of being called "gay." They shared their meager food and belongings even with those who had more than them. I'm crying now as I remember this. In the villages, Zimbabweans spoke to each other on the road, not just "Hi, how are you? I'm fine" then quickly get on their way. Instead, they also asked each person, "How is your family? How is your farm? How are your animals? How is life, etc.,? Their greeting in Ndebele language translates to, "How did you sleep last night?" This is a better question then asking a person how they are. Answering honestly how you slept includes whether sleep was refreshing with peacefully dreams or pain or worries or nightmares kept you awake. This was true "CP time" or colored people's time, because you got where you were going, whenever you got there. People are more important than your destination.

When you are ill and visit a traditional healer, you will be first asked, "How do you get along with your family? How do you get along with people in your village?"

Then they inquire about where your hurt is in your body or what's troubling you. Traditional healers were respected for their divination with "bones," and trance work, as well as use of natural medicines. I did not have to hide my psychic abilities. I could be all of my true self.

Ndebele Religion

I learned from the language and culture teacher that Ndebele people believe in the Creator and ancestors. Priest mediums are used as intermediaries to communicate with their ancestral spirits to give and receive messages. The Creator is seen as too great for people to go to alone. From further recent research of an article about the National Shrine Njelele, I read Zimbabweans come together as a nation to pray in times of disaster through ancestor spirits there. Only elders, ages 66 years and older, can pray for the nation. Matobo hills, a large area with two billion years old granite rock formations, has the National Shrine Njelele. Inside a cave with hidden tunnels, elders ask aloud for guidance for healing illnesses, settling disputes, and making political decisions. They ask what the people need to do and to learn in order to stop doing specific behaviors. These elders actually do hear answers. Therefore, the Njelele shrine is considered an oracle. Usually rituals are done at the shrine at the beginning of the rain season. And when the people did what the elder recommended for changes in their lives, then their requests are answered, such as for rain—it pours down raining.

Back in the village, I observed families come together to pray in their home compounds. My host family, the Dubes, held church in a hut. Other people came. The service began with European style hymns and reading from the Bible. I saw each person kneel and say a personal prayer aloud or singing.

Participation in the service, appeared egalitarian. Children had a large role in singing, leading, reading from the Bible, preaching, testifying and giving thanks. Women as well as men preached, danced, led songs, did healing. Later, the worship became traditional African. Men lead the dancing with boys carrying shepherds' staffs or tall sticks.

They start the day and end the day with prayer. All events begin and end with prayer. Meals begin with prayer. There were large churches of different denominations in the downtown city of Bulawayo. However, traditional spirituality, rituals, and honoring one's ancestors is still a larger aspect of Zimbabweans's lives.

Creatures Great and Small

One of the children came running into the kitchen hut to tell us there was a snake in the chicken house. The interpreter said usually the chickens sleep at night, but now they were squawking. Some snakes suck out the inside of eggs and then will use poison to kill the chickens. The family went together carrying big sticks. They set some wood on fire inside the fowl run of the chicken house. The snake ran out and the men hit and tried to burn the snake, but the snake went inside a hole. Somehow they got the snake out of the hole. When they threw the snake on the ground, in the large open yard between the huts, I was surprised at the size of the snake. It was a good two meters long. They were beating the snake with sticks and poking it. I thought it was dead but then the tail began to move. I pulled the small children and myself back further away, although we were way on the other side of the yard. The man used an ax to cut off the head, tail and then the body of the snake in half. The head and tail were saved, while the rest of the snake was taken into the fields and burned. The family said it was a black mamba snake — the second longest, most venomous deadliest snake in the world.

At night, I slept on the mud floor in the kitchen with the other women each on our own blankets, except I used a large army green rain poncho that opened up into a tarp, on top of that I had a foam mattress to cushion my protruding bones, and then blankets. I put my shoes at the end of my bed. One morning, I stuck my foot in my shoe and felt something cold and wet. Shaking my shoe, astonished as a large frog jumped out. From that day forward, I turn my shoes upside down before going to bed.

We were out for a walk, when I saw a giant millipede on the ground. At least giant to me, since in the United States millipedes look like a tiny black worm only an inch long. Shorter than an earthworm. For size, I asked if Mrs. Nube would put her hand next to it, so I could take a photo. She instead calmly put it on her hand. The millipede was as long as her hand, approximately six or seven inches! When I was younger, I didn't understand how centipedes could be bigger than a millipede and have longer legs. Doesn't centipede mean 100 legs and millipede mean 1000 legs? Actually house centipedes only have 30 legs. Millipedes have up to 300 legs.

Well, one afternoon Mehuli and I were sitting alone on the built-in bench along the wall of a hut. He was helping me study the Ndebele dictionary and language book. He looked up and told me not to move. When it was safe, he pointed out a large six-inch centipede up higher on the wall behind me but off to the side. We slowly got up and left the hut. Mehluli explained centipedes were poisonous in Zimbabwe! The big centipede looked like it had less legs, each with a hard, outer shell. Extremely different from the harmless, tiny, thin legs of the one and a half-inch-long centipedes in the United States. Later, I read that larger centipedes' bites can be very painful but only dangerous if you're allergic to them.

Chapter 21: Purpose for Being in Zimbabwe

Insight into my focus, purpose, and role for while I am in Zimbabwe?:

Metu Neter Cards: Auset hetep. I Ching: Hexagram 55 Abundance.

Auset is the universal archetype of the Mother. I was nurtured and cared for while I was in Zimbabwe. Perhaps because I was the only African American female in our ORAP class of eleven students, I was the only student given a "matron" while in the villages. There were four men from other African countries: one from Malawi and Ghana, and two from South Africa. By the way, the assumption that all Ghanaians were poor wasn't true, since this student told us he was from royalty, a prince, and paid his own way. The matron cooked my meals and provided boiled water for drinking, bathing, and washing my clothes. When in the village, I followed like a child, the matron's and the interpreter's directions, and went wherever they went. I did not know where we were going each day, because I didn't speak the language. Further, without streets nor street signs in the wide-open land between homes, I would be lost.

In Zimbabwe, you are not a woman unless you have birthed and raised children. Here I was, a woman in body, but had almost died twice when miscarrying babies. Am I not a woman?

It would have been difficult to explain this in a different language. Eventually, after several months when I became reasonably fluent with Ndebele language, the women insisted on having time alone with just the women to have conversations with me without my young male interpreter. Many topics were taboo to discuss with the opposite sex. It was the aunties, not mothers that discussed menstrual cycles and sex with daughters approaching puberty and adulthood.

The women in the villages were physically much taller, heavier weight, yet solid and stronger carrying the heaviest loads on their heads. Men did not come along and say, "Here give me that. Let me carry that for you." Men were shorter and thinner. They had the sexiest muscular body builds without forcing themselves to get up and go to the gym. They pushed the plows through the rocky soil and herded the goats and cattle over many miles. Men milked cows too.

Women carried almost everything on their heads. They carried water, bundles of firewood, heavy sacks of grains and mealie meal, furniture and tables. They fetched water from the rivers and bore holes. Occasionally the matron woke me very, very early in the morning to go with them to fetch water and small branches for firewood. Initially, they wouldn't ask or let me help carry the water. When they did let me try, I could only carry a small bottle of water a short distance as my head and especially my neck hurt. The second time, I was bravely able to carry a child size small bucket of water on my head all the way home. But I spilled water down one side of my dress. Embarrassed that now everyone would know I didn't know how to carry water! One of the women put leaves on the top of the bucket to prevent the water from spilling out of the bucket that I was carrying. My neck hurt for a whole week! I wondered how the women are able to do it. Perhaps it's because they start the girls very young therefore building up strength and endurance. There was a little girl five years old who came along. If I had learned to carry water and other things on my head as a young girl, I would have been strong enough to have carried the load of water with ease. Later, I learned if a girl could not carry a full jug of water on her head, then the amount of her loboda or bride's price dowry could be cut in half.

My interpreter Mehluli's mother, Mrs. Mhlope was assigned to be my matron. She carried my luggage from the bus to my home in the village. She slid and caught the heavy suitcase from the rack on top of the bus onto the top of her head. I chuckled in awe, because previously an older man fell over backwards trying to reach up to catch my suitcase with his arms. I had to catch both the suitcase before it fell and broke my camera, and the man. Most of the time my huge suitcase was hard for most men to carry in their hands, arms, or on their shoulders. Yet it seemed very easy for her to carry my luggage on her head. Her only complaint was that something in the bottom of my luggage was sticking her in her head. It was my deck of oracle cards.

I loved the bitter tiny green leaves that looked like the weeds, that my village home mother Mrs. Dube picked from the garden surrounding her home. She mixed it with onions, peanut butter, and a little red hot peppers. During the times that students returned to campus for classes, the cooks would occasionally cook the greens. They were surprised, frowning as they asked me, "You liked that?" Thereafter, the staff would give me bags of the dried greens that they didn't particularly want because the dried was, of course, several times more bitter than the fresh greens.

It was a relief when Mehluli told me I was not required to finish everything on my plate. In the United States, if you don't finish everything or most of what is on your plate, then the cook would be insulted and think you didn't like their cooking. If you acted as if you did like it and smiled, then it backfired on you because they would happily bring you a second helping! So in Zimbabwe, initially I was forcing myself to eat the huge servings of food given to me. Isitshwala is made out of finely ground white corn and cooked stiff similar to American grits is the Ndebele people's main staple food. There were times, of course, when the isitshwala got boring to me having to eat it several times daily, and some foods were foreign to my tastebuds which naturally I didn't like. Mehluli explained that the food I didn't eat from my plate was passed along to the next person in the hierarchy. The elders eat first, then the next person in age, until the children eat last. All very grateful to have what I didn't eat! That's why the plates given to me was piled so high with food.

Chapter 22: Stout?

"I want you to be stout." Mrs. Mhlope told me one evening.

What does stout mean? I asked Mehluli.

"Fat. She wants you to be fat. Do you want to be fat?"

Well, I said, "Not fat, just a little rounder."

Sounds simple enough. But little did I know what the implications were of having a matron who thought it was her duty to "make me fat."

Mrs. Mhlope arrived back in the village two days after I did. First thing she did was to ask me to make a shopping list. Then she sent someone the next day to buy the groceries. I should've known when they returned with 10 and 20 kilograms (20 to 50 pounds) bags of mealie meal, oranges, potatoes and more. The only items that were small, were the two tiny jars of peanut butter and that was only because the shop didn't have a larger size!

For breakfast it was porridge. Then barely two hours later she served "tea." Tea would've been fine alone, I could always use the extra fluids in the hot weather except she served me five or six small sweet potatoes with it, and sometimes groundnuts (peanuts) too. Then she would expect me to drink no less than 3 cups of tea. I was still stuffed from the large bowl of porridge. I don't know where she expected me to put all that food!

Everything she dished out for me and her son were in large serving bowls. She didn't seem to know the meaning of, "May I please just have a small amount?"

She would still fill the bowl piled to the top but not overflowing.

I tried for a week to convince her to not cook a large heavy meal for me after 6 PM. I was having stomach aches from the gassy potatoes or beans or in a tomato gravy she would serve after 8 o'clock at night. I would be tossing and turning and expelling gas all night. I don't know why she didn't notice as she slept on the mat next to me! The smell was offensive even to me. I would be irritable the next day from lack of sleep.

She then would say at 7:00 PM, "How about just some rice?"

"Okay, but just a little."

I agreed thinking okay rice is light. But I forgot with her there was no such thing as, 'just a little' and she really didn't know how to cook rice, it was always hard to chew.

We had just walked 16 km (10 miles) during the day therefore I was really too tired to think, let alone chew. I should've been hungry, but I was really too tired to eat. So I asked her to take some of the rice from the plate.

I ate it, which may have been a mistake because the next night she asked me again "Will you have rice?"

I agreed. "Yes, thank you."

What she gave me was a bowl of rice with chunks of potatoes with a little cooked chopped tomatoes and onions. Potatoes and rice was a strange combination to me and did not agree with my taste buds at that time.

After this incident, I refused to eat anything after 6:00 PM. The next night she came with a plate of isitshwala with cooked greens after I told her I would eat a few ground nuts and maybe an orange.

She asked, "What am I to do with the food I cooked? I am going to serve it to you for breakfast."

The next morning, I had porridge as usual. Porridge is thinned cooked white cornmeal. Mehluli said to me, "She's going to serve last night's dinner to you for lunch."

By then I thought it was going to be all dried out. But she didn't give it to me. So I worried she would give it to me for today's dinner.

Later he told me, "She fed it to the dogs."

I felt very guilty. Certainly, my conscious bothered me for wasting food, especially since food was scarce in Zimbabwe.

Really, she was only being like a good mother feeding me because I would be totally exhausted after walking all day, sometimes two hours walk towards and two hours from distant villages. Probably also slowing down their pace. Surely I must have been really skinny from burning more calories than I was taking in.

I did become stout. For the first time I had a "shelf" to rest my arms on my buttocks, under my enlarged breasts became chafed, and my thighs stuck and rubbed together when I walked. I had forgotten Auset's motherly energetic body shape is pleasantly plump. When my skin darkened from five months of sun rays unfiltered by pollution, Inviolatta proudly commented, "Now you look the way you are supposed to, African."

Chapter 23: Moving On

The Dema village community came out to see me off. I would be going to another village.

"Thank you for coming, and your good behavior. We wish you could stay and we wish you farewell. We will miss the times our groups have come together."

The best I could I responded, "I will miss being here too," as I tried to hold back the tears.

I was just starting to relax and enjoyed being there, as they told me I should do from the very first few days when

I arrived. I never really had to ask for anything. People here, have been very good to me and to each other while I've been here. They worked hard to teach me and show me about ORAP and to help me explore my interest in health. Life here is very busy and often difficult, yet they took time out to spend time with me and the rest of the community. Some walking very long distances. I did not have a chance to tell them how much I appreciated their inviting and welcoming me into their homes and community, because I had to go to the toilet and a delivery truck arrived at the Vice Chairman's home and the people left to help him. Perhaps this is good, because I would have cried throughout all of my giving thanks.

Second Village Stay

The first few days I was without an interpreter. I was surprised I could speak and understand more of the SiNdebele language than I previously thought. The people were also really excited to be able to speak directly with me. There was more interaction with the family this time. I got up earlier to help plant maize (corn) and bean seeds in evenly spaced holes, to cultivate and hoe the soil around the maize plants while removing weeds as we went along. We picked the indigenous green vegetable called olude. Some afternoons I went with them to fetch water and firewood. These activities gave me more time to talk with the family.

Mehuli tended to talk most of the time. I do learn a lot from him about the culture, farming, his life, etc. but from his perspective only of course. However, his talking to me also shut others out. This family made an effort to speak more English to me.

Glad there weren't males present, the women told me about child rearing and food taboos for children. One of the daughters said, "I am only expected to do domestic work as a career. I hate ironing."

I naïvely said, "There are other things you could do."

She asked, "Like what?"

I couldn't answer her. Not because she wasn't capable of doing other types of jobs but because she hadn't been exposed to other opportunities. I also couldn't answer her because I was thinking about all the domestic jobs I had simply because that is where older women told me I could get a job. Never mind that I took college prep classes and I wasn't dumb. Even in nursing school I excelled in the sciences in theory and medical technology, management, etc., but still nursing itself is traditionally a "women's job." And involves all of the chores male doctors wouldn't want to do.

She continued, "I was forced out of school because I had a baby. Pregnant women are expelled from school. But even so, the amount of work I'm required to do: breastfeed the baby, wash clothes every morning, cook, fetch water and firewood, clean the house, bathe the baby plus, work in the fields would prevent me from attending school."

My tongue was paralyzed. What could I really say? Here I was a foreign woman, a student doing what I wanted to do, resting on my laurels while she cooked and washed my clothes and cleaned up after me!"

A teenager asked me, "Do you know of a whitening cream to make my skin lighter so I can be light like you?"

I was shocked! I told her, "There are creams to lighten but not whiten skin. But why would you want to be white? I wouldn't want to be white because the ugliness of their harming people. Plus their skin ages sooner, sunburns and they have straight hair they can't do much with. I have the skin color I have not by choice, but because of white slave owners."

She said, "I understand because I read the books, Native Son, and also The Color Purple. Do you have a house girl?"

Laughing I told her, "No, in the United States, Black women are the house girls. There is no one to do anything for me except me."

Looking back as I write this book now, I am ashamed of how ignorant I was in my 40's. Realize now, they treated me as if I was a fragile white woman, gave me privileges without asking me if I needed or deserved these services. And I didn't know to pay them. This is what these Zimbabwean young women saw and wanted for their selves and their futures.

Several men told me, "You're to marry before you leave Zimbabwe."

Very scary! Especially after being told by one man that I was learning to be a Zimbabwean woman — to fetch water and firewood, to hoe, etc., — as he gave me a shovel to help dig, to find water for a well. This would've been okay if I wasn't hearing stories about some men drinking, not bringing money home, wife beating, everything is theirs' and demanding respect "in their home" when most of the time they were absent and didn't contribute to the labor and upkeep of the home. Sounded extremely familiar to me because I've been there and done that already in the United States. In Zimbabwe, while a few men stay in the village, most go to cities or to South Africa to work, only coming home on weekends, sometimes months or years later. I'm not blaming the men, that's what happens when colonizers come in and steal away your land, culture, values and dignity with forced labor or humiliating random underpaid employment.

And this matter of everyone telling me to get married or have a child "so as not to be lonely," why get married if I was going to be lonely anyway? In the United States, I'd have to work outside my home and neighborhood. Even in Zimbabwe, the workload doesn't allow for our idea of "quality time" with the children. However, infants and toddlers are carried on their mother's backs almost everywhere she or an older sibling goes. In the United States, we may work on the other side of the town or large city and put our children in the best school far away if we can afford it, or in daycare with strangers. I was afraid my children could grow up with problems or even hate me for a lack of bonding, love and genuine concern.

Comparatively, what I received in Zimbabwe was pure unconditional love.

Surrounding me, they truly made sure I didn't miss my family and friends too much. While Zimbabweans did not have an abundance of material resources, they shared whatever they had, along with an abundance of valuable priceless, healing caring and love. Hence, I experienced the meaning of hexagram 55: Abundance.

Chapter 24: Independent Study: Zimbabwe Healthcare

Students had to write out a learning contract listing their goals and how we were going to accomplish ORAP Zenzele College class assignments, as well as, research personal interests. We were to help the villagers do research on what was needed for their chosen projects, write down our observations, impact on us, and what we each personally wanted to investigate. At the end of the semester we were to write a ten-page paper that could be of use to the village and ORAP.

I also had to do written assignments to fulfill my independent study requirements for the School for International Training. Back then, access to a computer was rare. Therefore, I had several sheets of black carbon paper in my notebook to send copies of handwritten weekly reports to my academic advisor. Mail was very slow. She would receive my letters two to four weeks later, if at all.

Since my personal goal was to learn about the Zimbabwe healthcare system, I interviewed health care workers and villagers. I learned most villagers treated themselves with local herbs and prayers or went to traditional healers. The community health worker invited me to come along as she did her rounds in the village. I asked her, "How do you know when someone is ill? Do others tell you? Or does the patient send a message or a note with a child?"

She said, "I go door to door visiting, asking about people who are ill. Sometimes the sick person comes to my home. I go to visit people who are sick and see if their illness is mild or severe. If minor, I treat them with available tablets or pills. If severe, I take the person to the clinic or hospital."

Common illnesses she's seen were: headaches, stomach aches, diarrhea, complications of self-induced abortions, and pregnancies with twins and triplets.

At the clinic are the nurses. People called the head nurse "Sister" because she supervises the other nurses and staff. She wore an all-white dress and hat, similar to a navy uniform with stripes on her lapel and the shape of her hat. There were long waiting lines inside and outside the clinic. The doctor only visits rural clinics once a month and he only came to examine serious cases. Pregnant women go to the hospital by ambulance if there are problems. The Sister is the only trained midwife in the area. I accompanied her on home sanitation visits. She said she had already visited nine homes, traveling by foot, when I met her on the road. She checks inside each home for cleanliness of the toilet and kitchens, to see if the water containers are covered and the pot rack is high enough to protect it from animals and blowing dirt. Outside, she checks the cleanliness of the toilet, and that the rubbish pit is not overflowing and is divided into what can be burned and what could be composted for the garden.

Later, I joined the Sister at the Gwanda Outreach Baby Clinic outdoors in the village. Babies and young children were weighed in a hanging swing scale attached to a tree branch. Their weight in kilograms were recorded on a line graph on both the mother and the official yellow cards. I assisted with marking the mother's copy. Thirty-five children were in attendance. They were also given vaccinations for polio, measles, or diphtheria/tetanus/pertussis (DTP). Sister said last week no one came to the clinic, so she had to go to their homes and give baby vaccinations. She was glad to see the children at the outdoor clinic this week.

Ausar Auset Society Church introducing me to African culture and spirituality in the United States helped me to be more comfortable in the Zimbabwe villages. I also previously experienced being poor. All of my other study abroad classmates who were white, had difficulty adjusting and demanded to return home to finish out the year at their respective universities. I, instead, begged to stay in Zimbabwe to learn more about traditional healing.

Chapter 25: Traditional Healers

Two traditional healers introduced themselves and explained what traditional healers commonly do, and what they each did. Their stories were very similar. A traditional healer is a prophet (seer) with the ability to see the sick person, and what is wrong that is causing the sickness often before the sick person even comes to the door. When the sick person comes to their home, they will wait outside while the healer prepares to meet the person by making a protection. A protection for the healer and the healers' home if they see the sick person is carrying an evil spirit. I asked them questions about spiritual healing for behavioral as well as physical healing. Communication was difficult due to differences in culture, personal beliefs and points of reference. For example, I personally don't attribute problems to evil spirits. To improve communication, I showed them some of what I did as a healer.

During holiday break, I lived with these two women traditional healers; Mrs. Nube and Mrs. Moyo and their families. They had to get permission first from the village chief. He took several days to make a decision, but finally agreed. I insisted on not having a matron this time, which was also reluctantly granted. Mehuli still came along. I observed hem as they went about their daily chores and as we walked, they gathered herbs, they explained to me what the plants were used for. Many plants look like aloe vera to me. I wondered how the women could tell the difference since they told me some of these were poisonous!

One day, we walked to Mrs. Moyo's home where we were greeted, but then were left alone for a while in the empty hut. All of a sudden, we heard loud growls and the floor shook. Bursting through the doorway were the two traditional healers dressed in native attire with animal skins and feathers. Although I'd seen trance and spirit possession in rituals in the United States, I wasn't prepared for being so scared. Mehuli was trembling too, as we sat back-to-back on the mud floor holding tightly onto each other. We watched not knowing what would happen next. They seemed to be in trance with their eye gaze elsewhere. Eventually the two traditional healers left. Alone again, I asked Mehuli to explain. He said he had never experienced anything like this before. The two traditional healers returned, with their usual selves. We gradually calmed. They tossed the six small wooden piece "bones" divination to inquire about my family ancestors. However, I didn't understand most of what they were telling me of what the bones reading meant.

They also invited me to a special ritual another time at night where lots of n'angas came together. They sang and danced in line formations, stomping hard in Ndebele style with each n'anga holding a small sword. Later, as a going away present, they gave me my own sword, along with a small wooden mortar and pestle. All of these were symbols acknowledging me also being a traditional healer.

In turn, I invited them and their families to a small Auset ritual. I wore teal blue and white clothes. I started the ritual by pouring libation outside. Then the small group of healers and families went inside a hut. There I chanted the Auset mantra and went around the room hugging while briefly rocking each person as a mother would do to comfort a child. They had tears in their eyes and thanked me. We prayed for healing for our families and peace for the country.

Later, Mrs Nube told me the plants grew much bigger on the edge of the garden where I poured water for libation. Nonetheless, I was surprised when they later started referring patients to me. I also occasionally did oracle card and I Ching spiritual guidance for the traditional healers and patients. They asked me to name some of their babies, so of course I did destiny readings first.

During the second semester, I lived in Bulawayo. It wasn't the Spring semester because Zimbabwe is in the Southern Hemisphere, meaning their seasons are the reverse of in the United States. Therefore Christmas is in the summertime. Zenzele College teachers arranged for me to intern at Zimbabwe Traditional and Medicine Clinic. The medical doctor was British, the other health practitioners were local traditional healers n'angas, certified by the Zimbabwe National Traditional

Healer's Association, who had their own offices in the clinic.

N'angas are usually certified members of the Zimbabwe National Traditional Healers Association. Some practice on their own. They use herbal remedies, guided by a "healing spirit," and diagnose spiritual problems that have not yet become medical problems. Each specializes, therefore they will refer patients to other healers where needed or when their own method did not help.

As a registered nurse, I helped the British doctor examine patients, listen to their chests, monitor blood pressures and check their ankles for swelling. I taught the nurses' aides how to read a thermometer, feel for a pulse, count heartbeats, and use a stethoscope to check blood pressures. These were mostly patients with health insurance. The other patients went to see the traditional healers. I sat and observed the faith healer in her office across the hall. An n'anga showed me how she determined cause of and cured infertility without modern tests, medicine or surgery. I didn't understand most of what she was telling me because it was mostly invisible energetic healing. A male n'anga used herbs, and special prayers with rituals. Imagine seeing a huge python snakeskin stretched across the back wall in one of this n'anga exam room.

Zenzele College also arranged for me to train at a maternity clinic. The nurse midwife showed me how they determine how many weeks pregnancy by measuring the length of the woman's extended abdomen to her umbilicus navel since ultrasounds weren't available. Later I helped deliver a baby, coaching with breathing and trying to convince the nurse to allow the mother to sit up more rather than telling her push while lying flat on her back with her feet up in stirrups. There were some complications as the mother had bleeding from tears and the delayed delivery of the placenta. I showed the nurse natural ways of hastening the delivery of the placenta, by asking the mother to nurse the baby, but she was tired and in pain, so she refused. Instead I had to massage her nipples which gratefully successfully produced the placenta and the bleeding ceased. The grandmother thanked me afterwards and asked if they could name the baby girl after me.

Later, I attended an International Lay Midwife Conference with midwives from Denmark, Sweden, Australia, Canada and New Zealand, along with representatives from South Africa. The purpose of the midwife conference was to promote collaboration between Western trained medical doctors, nurses, and the lay midwives in the villages. Emphasis was on maintaining cleanliness during the birth to prevent infections with proper hand washing and sterile new razor blades to cut the umbilical cord. However, true collaboration meant acknowledging the wisdom of ancient traditional birthing methods. Allowing the mother to squat or get into whatever position was comfortable for the mother and the baby, instead of being forced to lie flat on her back on a table with her feet strapped to stirrups. Lying flat slows down the natural gravity descent of the baby and requires more hard pushing to get the baby out. Lay midwives knew what herbs to give and how to turn the baby in the womb to the head down position. European midwives complained about unnecessary medical procedures that harmed mother and baby such as excessive medicine induced labor and unnecessary cesarean sections. I told them about homeopathic remedies, such as Sepia, for postpartum depression and prolapsed uterus. Sepia naturally pulls the uterus back up into correct position and decreases the mother's fears or apathy about caring for the baby and her family after childbirth. It is possible the lay midwives already had similar herbs for this purpose. Due to language and cultural differences, it was difficult to communicate ideas.

***

Navigating downtown Bulawayo was easier because of street signs, as I went on my own to obtain health statistics from the education officer of the Ministry of education offices. English is the official language of Zimbabwe. It was wonderful having the familiarity of a downtown city to restore some of my independence as I rode buses and walked around.

I visited the modern city hospital and separate psychiatric hospitals. The buildings were small but similar to any hospital in the United States.

A couple of days each week, I went to a local n'anga and his young daughter Leticia's home in Bulawayo. They had a separate room attached to the house filled with shelves of assorted jars of herbs and other medicines. He was a tall, large man who always wore a long black dress. Everyone called him, "ubabamkhulu" which was confusing to me because the Ndebele name for God, "uNkulunkulu" sounded similar to my ears.

I spent most of this time in the medicine room learning from Leticia. She and I wore white. I was pleasantly surprised to see she also had drums! She showed me how to play special prayer rhythms on her drums. One day, her father excitedly ran inside the room saying, "It's raining! It's raining!" Since we have been waiting for rain for months, repeatedly disappointed when the skies would darken with clouds, yet no rain, I thought that's what he was excited about. Leticia explained to me that my playing the rhythm she taught me on her drums, caused it to rain!

Meanwhile, I lived with my former classmate Inviolatta at her home in Bulawayo. She lived in a large, beautiful three-bedroom brick ranch style home. Inviolatta shared her home with her sister and brother, a maid, and a girl from Botswana whom she helped to attend school in Zimbabwe. I slept in a twin-size bed with the maid. Similar to in the village everyone here helped each other.

When Inviolatta discovered I loved her steamed, buttered white pumpkin with the leaves, she prepared it often for me. Unlike in the United States, where we throw away the leaves, here everything is eaten, including most parts of animals. Okra leaves are cooked too. What I had difficulty getting used to was, the small servings of collard greens, only a couple of tablespoons on my plate, versus having a full bowl or two of cooked greens with the pot liquor to dip my cornbread in, like in the United States.

As you can see, being in Zimbabwe allowed me to experience the Metu Neter card Auset energy of the mother, fulfill the role of teacher, nurse, midwife, witness the ability to go into trance and purposely dream for guidance. I had to manage my emotions, not giving into indulgence as Zimbabweans were willing to give me anything I wanted.

Chapter 26: Before Colonization

In a bookstore in downtown Bulawayo, I found the book, <u>Guardians of the Soil: Meeting Zimbabwe's Elders</u>. Reading it helped me understand and believe the elders' stories about how Zimbabwe used to be before colonialism. In the chapter interview with the chief from Matabeleland in the southern area of Zimbabwe, he confirmed as the traditional healers previously told me, the land used to be very fertile, like a green rainforest. Instead of what used to be a large river, it had become so dry the villagers have to dig under the sand to get to the water. The white man's plow made rows deep into ground, as they cleared the land for fields and mining, causing the soil to be easily washed away. Animals and birds disappeared. In addition, whites killed off herds of wild animals, whereas the villagers only killed an animal when needed. Zimbabweans used to live in union and communion with their ancestor spirits and God. They believed the land only belongs to God and it was created for all the people to use. But when the whites came in, they took choice large areas of land and fenced it off as their own private property, and told the native people they had to buy land. Having no money, the African people were soon pushed off the land.

The elder emphasized that not having land destroys people's humanity.

Thereafter, too many people began dying from unknown diseases for which there was no cure. Previously, the traditional healers had herbs to cure every disease, but now with the drought, the trees, bushes, and plants are gone. In addition, harmony among the people was considered the most important for true health.

Elders see their God as superior to the Christian God especially in regards to, the concept of burning in hell for sins because Zimbabweans believe that everything and everyone can be forgiven. They had forgiveness rituals whenever there were disputes between people. Therefore the idea that God is not forgiving doesn't make sense.

Other elders in the book, added that their Creator did not have heaven or hell since the dead do not die. Christian missionaries taught them that acknowledging their ancestors was evil, so now their ancestors' voices are not heard.

Zimbabweans also had utmost respect for women, especially their mothers. The womb of a woman is a shrine. A man is only successful because he consults a woman. And if he is beating his wife he is a coward, and in doing so is also disrespecting his parents. Getting angry with or raising his hand to his mother will cause him to be cursed.

Whites brought greed and taught greed and individualism to young people in their schools. Children don't listen to elders nor know their history and culture of how to live in harmony with each other and nature. Along with the land drying up, so did the people's dignity, independence and sense of responsibility.

As I read the book, <u>Guardians of the Soil: Meeting Zimbabwe's Elders</u>, my heart was filled with both awesome love and sorrow for the people, culture and land of Zimbabwe. I bought two more copies of the book, gave one copy to my village family for the children, and gave the other copy to Mehluli. I urged and hoped the book would inspire him to write his own book about the many fascinating stories he told me of village life.

Chapter 27: Personal Reflections and Struggles Living in Zimbabwe

While in the village, I'd been wanting to write freely for days, weeks, months. My Zimbabwean family tried to read everything I wrote. Have they not heard of a journal or diary which has a person's private thoughts and is kept locked at all times except for when writing in them? I really needed a creative outlet. I couldn't even cook without other people interrupting as if I didn't know how to do anything. Never mind, that I was almost 42 years old. Otherwise, I was just sitting around staring at other people sitting and talking to each other, except when we were doing chores. They seemed honored to remove all tasks from my hands. This was literally very, very boring. I'd sit there thinking of all the other things and responsibilities I had to do, like school assignments.

Later, by the questions they asked me, I began to understand Mehuli, and the few other young people who could read some English, were watching me write in my notebook because they had not seen anyone write in cursive before. They did not join their letters together. My writing was even more mysterious because I wasn't doting my i's nor crossing my t's as I tried to write as fast as I could, transcribing the history or stories the elders were telling me. While taking notes in college, I had gotten into the habit of going backwards later, after a couple of sentences to cross my t's and dot my i's. I didn't realize this was foreign to them, until Mehuli asked as he pointed at my notebook, "Oh, is this a t? Oh, that must be two t's." I showed him, by first writing each letter separately and then making small strokes to join the letters that I was doing the same as he prints. Cursive writing can be faster than printing after you get used to it. My worries that they were spying on me were unfounded since they couldn't read my handwriting. They were only curious.

Even having some time to just sit and reflect, composing my many conflicting thoughts would have been wonderful and worthwhile. But where? Whenever I tried to get some quiet time here, someone comes knocking to ask if I'm sick, or to tell me to come and cook or bathe. The husband of the family and Mehuli seemed to think it was their job to criticize whatever I did. "You can't cook. You can't wash pots." They never even let me get started, to see what I can do or what I know how to do already. Like with the drums, the men criticized and then left, but the women and I enjoyed playing the drums together.

Zimbabwean sit, stand and sleep close together. They do the same with strangers. Shoulder to shoulder. If they like you, they will grab your hand while walking. There is a shortage of transportation so when riding in any vehicle, expect to be packed in like sardines. There is no difference where men or women sit. I had to get used to sitting partially on men's thighs occasionally, or even have a man leaning on me. Having to sit in the boot of a commuter omnibus minivan or the back of a pickup truck, especially in your Sunday best gets interesting.

Coming from a family and a society that does not touch much, I had to get used to the Zimbabwean close personal space. Sometimes I was embarrassed, not quite sure of the other person's intentions. Usually the innocent touches were brief similar to how young children touch while they talk. I got used to the closeness, but I found it hard to initiate touching. Sitting close did not bother me much except with men, since I was raised as a Muslim.

Having other people handling, and at times going through "my" belongings is something I never quite got used to. I always felt shocked and annoyed, although the intensity of my feelings decreased with time.

Collectivism was both an area of my keen interest and a source of frustration, as I struggled to balance the advantages of collectivism with my perception of it being seeming rigid as compared to United States' individualism freedoms of privacy, own opinions, questioning, and wandering from place to place. I was raised in a Black American extended family, in a segregated collective neighborhood. As a result of racism and discrimination, parents couldn't allow their children to have an opinion nor choices. Therefore, as an adult I cherished my "independence" although it could be lonely and isolating.

Mrs. Mhlope would tell me when to get up in the morning, when to take a bath, and then inspect me while saying, "You didn't wash your lower legs and feet." Or, "How could you have bathed without a towel?"

I was afraid of taking my shoes off in the concrete outhouse because I didn't want parasitic worms to enter through my feet. I hoped she wouldn't come into the outhouse and inspect me while I had no clothes on but she didn't, unless she peeked.

She would tell me, "Your clothes and shoes are dirty. Take them off, so I can wash them."

They wouldn't let me do anything, so I wondered how could my clothes be dirty? Usually, in the United States, I would wear my clothes two days before I washed them. My socks and underwear I would otherwise change daily. Here they wash everything including backpacks and purses. Perhaps, it is because of the dry dirt roads scattering dust everywhere.

When I returned to Zenzele College campus in the city of Bulawayo, the other students told me they experienced similar from their host families. Some were told to bathe two or three times a day even though the family didn't bathe as often. I imagine the white students' skin might appear dirtier. It was explained Zimbabweans treat all visitors that way. Visitors should be able to rest since they work hard at their own homes. One of the African students from Malawi told us, that this was also true in his country. They just want the visitor to be comfortable and to have the best the family can offer, even if they go without the items or services themselves.

There were times when I cried quietly in my bed because all my time was planned by someone else, even going to a church on Tuesday, Friday and Saturday nights and from noon to 4 PM on Sundays. There was no privacy, I couldn't even go to the outhouse by myself. Sometimes I refused to go to church because some services would begin late at night, it was all in the Ndebele language, and Mehuli since he was a male he sat on the other side of the church with the rest of the men. I was given an English Bible to read while they read the same verses over and over again from week to week.

Sometimes when I stayed back in the hut, because I had awful headaches with heavy menstrual bleeding. They asked me, "Aren't you afraid to be alone?"

I simply told them, "No."

But really, I was just so glad to get a chance to rest, to just think and reflect. They didn't realize how exhausting it was to have to try to interpret and understand everything anyone said or did.

This is how the hexagram 17 Following's advice for deciding to participate in the Zimbabwe Organization Rural Association Progress (ORAP) SIT Study Abroad Program, unfolded all the while I was in Zimbabwe. I had no choice but to humbly follow along in the yielding role of Auset. I didn't know the rural area, language, laws, nor culture. Never thought to run away. How could I anyway?

Chapter 28: Americans Over Concerned About Cleanliness, Germs and Illness?

When I went to the villages, after a while, I began to question my beliefs about cleanliness, germs and illness. Is what we were taught about hygiene and disease true? There is such a total lack of concern about the transmission of the invisible bugs and other organisms we call germs. I rarely saw the people in the village wash their hands except for before meals, when everyone shares the same large bowl, passed from person to swish our hands. But I cringed knowing we used the toilet, even the public toilets in the city didn't have soap, worked in the fields, changed diapers, polished the floor with cow dung, milked the cows, and handled other animals before putting our hands in the same bowl, and dried with the same towel that is passed around to everyone in the room. After eating, the same towel was then used to dry the dishes. This was upsetting to watch.

I asked to have my water boiled, as was advised by the School for International Training's nurse and in the health document she gave us, and then wondered why I still became ill. Fortunately, I only had mild stomach cramps, headache, and brief diarrhea for a couple of days. I asked for boiled water for washing my hands after that and refused to use the towel. It wasn't until much later, I observe the "dishwashing" methods. Culturally, they insisted on visitors not washing dishes. I let it be, since I hadn't gotten seriously ill, although some of my classmates did get serious diarrhea and dehydration. When the women washed dishes and pots outside, they used the river water and the sand for scrubbing. No choice but to use the same water the chickens, dogs and goats have walked and relieved themselves in. When they could fetch water from the borehole wells, that we were told it was safe water for us to drink they also used sand to clean the inside and outside of the large metal can they used to carry the water. When I asked a young woman about this, she said the sand removes the rust." After that, I insisted on boiled water even if it was from the boreholes.

And I assumed my hand-washing water was from the borehole well but weeks later Mehuli who usually helped me wash my hands said, "You've been using river water before now. Why are you upset?"

I was shocked, of course, thinking I had explained the rationale and expressed my dissatisfaction to Mehuli, as my interpreter, many times. He himself didn't use soap even if I brought it to the table. He showed me plants they rub their hands on that is like a soap. Weeks later, he did use the diluted commercial dishwashing liquid with me when we washed our hands outside. I should've known because he asked me several times, "Wouldn't you get used to the water in Zimbabwe? It is hard for people who live there to understand, since the water doesn't seem to make them ill.

Yet their babies often have "running stomachs." Perhaps they think diarrhea in babies is normal not an illness.

Leftover food from the prior evening's meal, served on plates was left in the oven overnight and eaten the next morning. There weren't refrigerators in the rural areas. But I thought it odd to see the same practice in the city where there are refrigerators available. Eggs are not refrigerated.

People became defensive when I tried to teach about the concept of bacteria. Someone at the clinic mentioned she didn't believe in germs. The water and the food didn't seem to make them ill. Perhaps because they were probably better nourished, rested more because when the sun went down, they went to bed. They were very strong and

CHAPTER 28: AMERICANS OVER CONCERNED ABOUT...

hard-working and could outwork me many times over in just a single day.

I thought I had made a conscious choice to not waste or over consume the Earth's resources, but here I was being made to live up to their image of how rich person should live. Meanwhile, I was thinking of people who didn't have clothes or soap or water to wash clothes or bath every day. This was hard to explain to them. I tried explaining that more is not always better when the matron insisted that I add more and more laundry powder in addition to the laundry detergent already in the large plastic basins, where the water was already full of thick, sticky suds. Probably from seeing the extra bubbles in television advertisements. Then the soap would be hard to rinse out, because of the drought, there wasn't enough water to rinse the clothes well, so the rinse water was also very soapy. Since they immediately dumped the wash water into the garden or around the lemon and other fruit trees, to me they were poisoning the soil. In America, fish were dying in the lakes from chemical pollution.

Reality

This again shows how naïve and privileged I was to even think this way. Water and firewood to boil my water was scarce, plus it wasn't on my sore back, feet, and neck that the water was carried. Why was I being so picky? Did my then 86-year-old grandmother, not tell me stories about when there wasn't running water in the United States? She used to wash her hair in streams. People still had ice boxes in the city when

I was a little girl in Philadelphia. Her family lived through the Great Depression when almost nobody had anything. My grandmother would cook for our family reunions throughout the day before and during the night. There wasn't enough room in the refrigerator for all the food, so it sat out all night and all the next day at the picnic. Nonetheless, we didn't get sick.

Chapter 29: Vegetarian Dilemma

What do you do when you are the honored guest or one of several guests, and the hosts goes out of their way to prepare a meal especially for you? However, the food is not something you usually eat, or in some cases would rather not eat. In the village, the host places a big serving bowl of meat in front of you, after all you are one of the honored guests. You have been vegetarian for six years, not for any philosophical reasons but because whenever you would eat meat your stomach revolts and gives you a terrible stomach aches for two days straight, during which time you couldn't eat any other food even if you wanted to. Prior to this you had eaten meat all your life, except for pork having been raised Muslim. You had sausage, bacon, steak for breakfast. Bologna, pastrami, salami, and other cold cut deli or corn beef sandwiches, hamburgers, or fried chicken for lunch. Meatloaf, pot roast, turkey, goose, duck, lamb, veal or goat for dinner. At barbecues, you would have several pieces of each type of meat among the hotdogs, burgers, chicken, and ribs from the grill.

Perhaps your difficulty digesting meat was because of the additives, hormones and antibiotics they gave to the animals in the United States. You happen to have seen the 20/20 episode on television where a Food and Drug Administration worker was fired because he insisted on discarding chicken that showed signs of salmonella, some gross with green pus. He would put the infected chicken in the trash bin, then someone would come behind him and put the chickens back on the assembly line, cut out the obvious green pus spots, and send the infected chicken to the markets. Since then you have bought and eaten only kosher meat but later your stomach won't allow you to eat Kosher nor halal meat. Kosher chickens are very different in appearance, texture and taste them regular chickens at the supermarket. It has better flavor. Yet, perhaps a chicken is still a chicken in the United States, and the rabbi just says a prayer over the chicken, kills it humanely and sells it.

So now you are a vegetarian and a couple years later, you meet and join a religious group that promotes being vegan. This group has all kinds of logical reasons why humans shouldn't eat meat: If we were meant to eat meat we would have the same type of intestines carnivorous animals have, but instead our intestines are longer with extra pockets that meat gets trapped in and takes too long to digest and rots inside us. Hence the high incidence of colon cancer. If we were meant to eat meat, we would have fangs and other types of specialized teeth. We would salivate at the sight and smell of a fresh killed animal, eating it right then and there, getting excited about the warm blood dripping down our chins. If we were meant to eat meat, we wouldn't have to cook it to tenderize it or to kill bacteria or parasites. Carnivorous animals don't have to worry about getting sick from bacteria. Nor do they do add seasonings like salt, pepper, onion, garlic, green pepper, parsley, etc. to make it taste like a vegetable.

All of these reasons made perfect sense to you. And after years of not eating meat you don't even crave it. Except you did eat fish every once in a while. Then this year, you get tired of being tired all the time, your hair coming out in your comb, and feeling hungry all the time. A couple of your friends who belong to the vegetarian group that are supposed to be vegan eat chicken and fish. They serve fish at their home and you decide to join them since fish is the one flesh you crave. You do okay with the fish, except later you notice you become constipated and can even have a queasy stomach if you indulge in more than a small amount. Since you have been a vegetarian you have not suffered from constipation usually having two to three healthy bowel movements daily. Previously you had a bowel movement once every three days and sometimes only once a week, while growing up eating meat.

You've also read Ayurvedic medicine advises that vata constitution or slender built people are the only people who need to eat meat in order to stay grounded, otherwise they are too spacey. But you also read in the same book, vata type people have a hard time digesting food even raw vegetables, so this seems contradictory to you. So you decide to eat fish only occasionally, once every one to two weeks.

Then you sat in the first Environmental Studies class of the semester at The School for International Training, and the teacher hands you, out of all the other students, an article on fish — about how ocean fish is now being farm raised basically the same way beef is raised. Meaning fish such as salmon can be fattened or made lean to order and given antibiotics. You were shocked but you really should not have been. You thought only catfish was farm raised. Therefore you stop eating fish for a while, and then selectively occasionally.

The following summer, you feel constantly hungry. Nothing you eat is appealing or satisfying. It is hard to even think of anything exciting to eat. Now you hear in conversations with people who are from Africa, or have been there, that everyone eats meat, especially in Zimbabwe where you're going and therefore you will starve. As a result, you decide that you will eat meat, when you get there. Besides, the meat comes from free roaming cattle and chickens without additives. But now you are here, in the village, the host places a big serving of meat in front of you. After all, you are one of the honored guests. You don't want to offend your hosts, so you pick a piece of meat from the bowl and put it in your mouth. It tastes like liver and you remember that the liver's job is to clean the blood. You want to spit it out, but you don't. You take another piece from the other side of plate and it tastes more like beef, but it still tastes very much like flesh to you. Same with the pieces of chicken served in another meal. Somehow the idea that it is a leg you are biting into, is repulsive therefore only two bites is all you can manage. Why after having been a meat eater most of your life, why are you so sensitive to the sight, smell, taste and thought of meat? You push yourself to eat a little anyway. On the last day in the first village you have stomach cramps, headache, dizziness and nausea. Finally, your hosts tell the guests, after three of the four other students are also ill with these same symptoms plus diarrhea, that you do not have to eat anything you don't want to eat. They don't want you to get sick. By that time, you're too nauseated and sick to want to eat anyway. When you return to campus you rest your stomach for a day or so and then you try again to nibble on the chicken at mealtimes, rationalizing you need to get used to eating meat before you return to the village.

CHAPTER 29: VEGETARIAN DILEMMA

Several months later, near the end of the time you're in Zimbabwe, you are invited to your friend's house for the weekend. She prepares beans for you, but you are surprised when she serves you a large chicken leg on the same plate. You eat it because she's watching your every move. You tell her it has nice flavor she has seasoned it well. But looking at that leg! The next meal she serves you fish. You try to refuse by telling her that you thought she had prepared that plate for someone else. She looks very disgusted, so you say you will have a small piece. The fish is in a sauce but you can still see the head and the eyes. You eat a small piece and your friend slides the rest of the fish onto your plate.

She later serves you cuddled milk, that she says she loves, and other

Zimbabweans have said it is their favorite food that's usually served for dessert. Someone had made it especially for her for the occasion of you being there. She is again is watching you closely, so you eat it slowly.

She asked you, "How do you like it?"

You say, "I will have to get used to it."

Upon which she serves you more. The curdled milk was so sour and fermented it burns your tongue. You eat it but you were feeling trapped and angry at yourself and at you friend. You like your friend very much, which puts more pressure on you than it did in the village to conform to another culture's food tastes.

You are confused because your friend knows you have food allergies and have been vegetarian for years and had urged you several times to tell the campus kitchen your needs. Perhaps she thinks maybe the food allergies are because the United States has too many additives, pesticides, hormones and antibiotics. Some Americans won't eat meat for political and philosophical reasons but even international people when they come to the United States stop eating meat. Here in Zimbabwe in the rural areas the meat is fresh. You value the friendship and don't want to argue, knowing your friend probably would not understand and would only feel hurt. Cultural shock and homesickness began to settle in, and you are depressed for most of the following week. You're not homesick because you miss your family and friends in the United States. You are homesick for your own home where you can cook your own food, and to have some semblance of a familiar routine.

What would you do? Would you decide to give up meat again, even the fish? After all they serve you plenty of fresh roasted groundnuts for breakfast and snacks. Is it necessary to eat meat protein at each meal? Would you give in, to fit in?

Actually, eating meat in the village was rare because of the drought. The cows and the chickens were very skinny pecking at the few blades of grass and seeds. Zimbabweans ate reconstituted dried fish and mopane worms that are giant caterpillars. Meat was only served on special occasions. I guess in the cities, the people are rich in comparison since our student handbook had the following: "Matebeleland is cattle country and the town specialty is beef. Many

Zimbabweans will not eat anything else, and steak is therefore invariably found on the menu at any restaurant, regardless of its theme. Bulawayo steak houses are famous for their generous portions of tender prime beef and most of them serve a Texan-style plank steak that defies all but the very largest of men."

Therefore, I Ching hexagram 21 literally meant "biting through" as I did have to make myself bite through the meat, mopane worms and dried fish. Oh, and even the organic beans. Taught as a teenager to "pick" beans by finding and throwing away tiny clumps of dirt, rocks, or misshapen broken beans. Well, while assisting the cooks in the kitchen, they gave me a bag of beans to pick. I began picking out the small beetles quickly discovering, as the cooks laughed at me, that there were as many dried beetles in the bag as there were dried beans. Knowing how precious food was, I took out the debris but left in the beetles. After cooking, they added flavor, were actually delicious and gave a nice crunch! Of course, I had plenty of other experiences to bite through.

Chapter 30: Reality of the Situation

Actually, Hexagram 21 is more about correcting or punishing someone for criminal behavior in the community. I personally, not that I know of, did not have a situation where I needed to punish anyone. However, while I was in Zimbabwe in November 1997, and for three days in January 1998 there were protests and food riots because of the unaffordable higher prices of necessities such as food staples of cornmeal, cooking oil, rice, bread, and gasoline for travel. Rioters broke into shops and delivery trucks to take mostly food items. Violence erupted as rioters overturned commuter omnibus minivans blaming the drivers for higher fares. The government harshly punished demonstrators, injuring them by beating, tear gas, and shooting some people. Those in jail received inhuman treatment although the Zimbabwe Constitution prohibits torture, cruel and inhuman treatment. The police were overwhelmed and unprepared calling in the military to help as there had not been previous riots of this magnitude. Allegedly, there was also some political corruption and violence against the opposition.

Unknown to me, there was also a global economic crisis occurring that started July 1997 with the Asian Financial Crisis as monetary currency became devalued in first Thailand, then Indonesia, South Korea, Malaysia, Hong Kong and Japan. This led to slowdowns in manufacturing, increased unemployment, bankruptcies, oil and food shortages which also caused political instability and riots in Asia. Previously, Zimbabwe's economy had been considered stable with combined subsistence and commercial agricultural farming, when it had a food surplus during the drought years. However this changed with increasing inflation, taxes, the government's huge civil service job sector amidst raising unemployment with low wages in other sectors. Therefore labor strikes occurred, including on commercial farms, with demands for lump sum payouts to disabled war veterans and more. Zimbabwe's currency exchange rate dropped 75%. As you can see, the reasons for the food riots, inhuman punishment of the rioters, yet leniency of punishments for incorrigible government corruption were complicated.

The ORAP Zenzele College closed for the next semester as American students complained about poorer quality of the class lectures and increasingly absent teachers. Wow! How ignorant we students were of the extent of the teachers', their families' and the country's struggles. Even oblivious to risks to our own safety, as we regularly traveled downtown.

Again, I apologize for my ignorance then and now. I wrote these chapters about Zimbabwe from my personal experience, diaries, class notes, and the college student handbook. After currently reading memoirs in 2022, written by people who grew up in Zimbabwe I see there is plenty history and daily life I didn't know, that I couldn't know because of language and cultural barriers. The books I read were written by people from northern Zimbabwe. Even in the north there are many more tribes and languages besides Shona and siNdebele along with those of people who immigrated from bordering countries. Zimbabwe was only fifteen years post War of Independence while I was there in 1997. Many were recovering from memories of war atrocities, torture, rape, servitude and pillage by the British and also from other native Zimbabweans.

All this I didn't know. If I had known, I would have been more compassionate and helpful. Regretfully, I didn't know how to send money to Zimbabwe. Inviolatta warned me that sending anything through the mail risked theft or her paying bribes for her to retrieve it from the post office. Cost of postage from the United States was also outrageously expensive, as I found out when I tried to send diapers and sewing supplies. I wish I had given more money while I was in Zimbabwe and also after I returned to the United States, but I soon became caught up in my own survival struggles.

Books and Articles Mentioned in This Book

I purposely did not write this book in a scholarly way, with huge academic words, book quotes and citations. This is because we all have this knowledge and information within us. Books are just one way to share and communicate with each other. I believe there really is no such thing as an expert, it is simply one person sharing their opinion and experiences. The so-called expert may have done the research and statistics to find how many other people might agree. And they had the money and the time to get published. But life is always changing. Meaning what was true two weeks ago, may not be true today. And the authors may live in a completely different situation than yours, and therefore the advice may make no sense for your current life situation. Books are a way to have a long-distance conversation. Often with a stranger. But there is enough commonalities, so that we don't feel alone. Here is a list of books whose authors think similar to my experiences, and some who don't.

African Names: The Ancient Egyptian Keys to Unlocking Your Power & Destiny. Hehi Metu Ra Enkamit. (1993). Ser Ap-uat Press.

Black Panther (2018). Movie. PG-13.

Guardians of the Soil: Meeting Zimbabwe's Elders. By Chenjerai Hove and Ilija Trojanow (1996). Baobab Books.

Heading Towards Omega: In Search of the Meaning of the Near-Death Experience. By Kenneth L. Ring. (1984). HarperPerennial.

I Ching: A New Interpretation for Modern Times. By Sam Reifler (1974).

I Ching: The Tao of Drumming. By Michael Drake. (1991). Talking Drum Publications. (paperback). Random House Publishing Group. (e-book).

I Ching Praxis: Forty Years of Practical Insights into the I Ching. By Ra Un Nefer Amen (2014). Khamit Media Trans Visions, Inc.

Light Emerging: The Journey of Personal Healing. By Barbara Ann Brennan. (1993). Bantam Books.

Medicine Cards: Revised, Expanded Edition. By Jamie Sams and David Carson

(1988, 1999). New York: St. Martin's Press.

Medicine Cards: The Discovery of Power through the Ways of Animals. By Jamie Sams and David Carson (1988, 1999). New York: St. Martin's Press.

Metu Neter Cards. By Ra Un Nefer Amen (1990). New York, Khamit Corporation.

Metu Neter Vol. 1: The Great Oracle of Tehuti and the Egyptian System of Spiritual Cultivation. By Ra Un Nefer Amen (1990). New York, Khamit Corporation.

Ochosi: Ifa and the Spirit of the Tracker. By Awo Fa'lokun Fatunmbi (1992). Original Publications.

Organization of Rural Associations for Progress ORAP Zenzele College Student

Handbook, Grassroots Development and NGO Management 6. (August 18, 1997).

Sacred Path Cards: The Discovery of Self through Native Teachings. By Jamie Sams (1990). New York: HarperCollins Publishers.

Sacred Path Workbook: New Teachings and Tools to Illuminate Your Personal Journey. By Jamie Sams (1991). New York: HarperCollins Publishers.

The Astrology of I Ching. (1976, 1993). By W. K. Chu and W. A. Sherrill. Penguin Books.

The Forgotten Child of Zimbabwe. By Debra Chidaka Akue (2017). Christian Faith Publishing.

The I Ching or Book of Changes. By Richard Wilhelm and Cary Baynes. (1950). Princeton University Press.

The Harlem River Arrangement: The I Ching Transcripts. By Ra Un Nefer Amen. (1984).

The Illustrated I Ching Workbook. R. L. Wing. (1987). Aquarian Press.

The Medicine Woman: Inner Guidebook: A Woman's Guide to Her Unique Powers Using the Medicine Woman Tarot Deck. (1991, 2012). By Carol Bridges. U.S. Games Systems, Inc. Stanford, CT 06902.

The Illustrated I Ching Workbook. R. L. Wing. (1987). Aquarian Press.

Zimbabwe Country Report on Human Rights Practices for 1998. U.S. Department of State. https://1997-2001.state.gov

Zimbabwe Human Rights NGO Forum: A Consolidated Report on the Food Riots 19-23 January 1998. Report Compiled by the AMANI Trust on Behalf of the Zimbabwe Human Rights NGO Forum.

Zulu Bone Oracle. By Ulufudu (1989). Wingbow Press.

Author's Bio

Haneefa Mateen has a wealth of life experiences and knowledge from exploring healing methods for mind, body and soul. A natural teacher, healer, and artist she shares more of her wisdom in her second book, Decisions Decisions: Getting Answers to Life's Challenges. This is Volume 1: Getting Started. The first volume of five volumes in an accessible, easy on the eyes, large print format.

She has an associate's degree in registered nursing, bachelor's in International Studies, master's in Rehabilitation Counseling, and a doctorate in Clinical Psychology. She currently does spiritually integrated therapy and healing, and is active in African American community cultural events.

www.ingramcontent.com/pod-product-compliance
Lightning Source LLC
Chambersburg PA
CBHW020522080526
44583CB00013B/698